SO-BTZ-375

A DEER IN
THE LOBBY

George,

Tel Adrianne This is "must" reading. Enjoy. W LV

A DEER IN THE LOBBY

*an irreverent look
at american management*

by
WHIT SPAULDING

BARN PRESS : Birmingham, Michigan

Illustrations by Doug Spaulding

Copyright © 1991 by Whit Spaulding

All rights reserved. No part of this book may be reproduced or transmitted in any form or by any means, electronic or mechanical, including photocopying, recording or by any informational storage or retrieval system — except by a reviewer who may quote brief passages in a review to be printed in a magazine or newspaper — without permission in writing from the publisher. For information contact Barn Press, 6397 Sunningdale, Birmingham, MI 48010.

Publisher's Cataloging in Publication Data

Spaulding, P. Whitney, 1929-

    A deer in the lobby
    1. Business - Management

HG5095   658.4'01   90-84225

Library of Congress Catalog Card Number: 90-84225

ISBN: 0-9627813-0-4 (Hardcover)
ISBN: 0-9627813-1-2 (Paperback)

Printed in the United States of America

READ THIS FIRST

Barb, my secretary, called me at home and said, "THERE'S A DEER IN THE LOBBY." That was in the spring of 1988, and I immediately thought, "I'm going to write a book about my hospital experiences." This is it.

At the time I was the interim chief executive officer of a rural hospital in northern Michigan. I went into the hospital and found that the deer hadn't hurt anyone when he crashed through the glass doors of the lobby, but we had to call the Sheriff's Department to escort the deer off the premises.

More crazy and humorous and fascinating things happen in hospitals than anyplace else, and I am compelled to share some of the more bizarre experiences and insights with you: whether you work for an insurance company, an Air Force squadron, or a building contractor. They don't teach this stuff in schools, so I hope you newcomers may learn a thing or two. And you old-timers can always sharpen your management style.

I suggest you skip through the book and read a few chapters that sound interesting. I hope you are amused or annoyed at some of the observations. If you don't get a chuckle or learn something from this book, let me know and I'll send your money back.

Hospitals are often the scene of tragedy, most often affecting human beings. It is important that hospitals (and all businesses) are well managed and geared to caring and service. It is also important to keep a sense of humor - I hope this book helps.

Dave Benfer
Helen Boyden
Ed Connors
Noreen Davis
Barb Donaho
Ginger Droz
Sy Gottlieb
Barb Gomolak
Stewart Hamilton
S. Corita Heid
Bill Hochkammer
Vic Ludewig
John McGibony
Walt McNerney
Duane Newland
Phil Partington
Karl Scharff
Peg Schumaker
Polly Spaulding
John Stewart
Pat Tavidian
Robert Townsend
Barney Tresnowski
Jim Varnum
Peter White

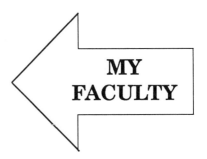

MY FACULTY

THANKS,

Whit

CONTENTS

CONTENTS

CONTENTS

CONTENTS

"Brevity is the Soul of Wit"

Shakespeare, Hamlet - 1601

"Brevity is the Soul of Whit"

Abel, Schumaker - 1981

ADVERTISING

Advertising in the media has become an important dimension of hospital operations.

A sage trustee told me, *"Promise less than you deliver."*

I've known hospitals that have turned out TV commercials trying to compare themselves to the Mayo Clinic, and everyone (public, docs, employees, trustees) knows that is poppycock. Don't do it.

The most effective advertising is done by your staff. Every time they do a good job, the patients and public will know it. Then let word of mouth be your main advertising medium.

A.I.L. PAPER

Here comes some really bad news. Hospitals, and most other businesses, are being inundated with "A.I.L. paper."

The definition of "A.I.L. paper" is: *those documents you generate to keep the following groups employed:*
  A - Accountants
  I - Inspectors
  L - Lawyers

Accountants have to establish a "paper trail" to satisfy the various payors and auditors that the hospital is playing by the rules of Medicare, Workers Comp., Aetna, Medicaid, Blue Cross, Kaiser, etc.

Inspectors believe only what they see on paper. They must see written policies, rules, and definitions; and then match them up with written records of performance. For example, the policy that says the auxiliary generator will be tested every week must be matched by a log that indicates a date and initials to "prove" the policy was carried out. Why don't the inspectors just watch the generator being tested and ignore all the paperwork?

Lawyers insist on documenting everything. In order to terminate an employee a huge stack of documents is needed to justify the action. Most of the time the documents have little or nothing to do with the real reason for termination, but it is necessary to satisfy the judicial process.

I remember when the medical record was a neat way for the doctor to communicate with the nurse and vice versa, so together they could care for the patient. No more! The medical record has become A.I.L. paper.

Businesses are choking on A.I.L. paper, thanks to copy machines, fax machines, and computers. The only good news I can think of relating to this disaster is to invest your money in the paper manufacturers - they have a prosperous future.

ANNUAL MEETINGS AND REPORTS

Sure you have an annual meeting for the trustees (stockholders), and you probably have some affair for the big-shooters like the Medical Staff. BUT the groups that are often neglected are the employees and the public.

The public must receive some sort of accounting of how their hospital is doing. After all it is their hospital (perhaps not legally), and they deserve an annual report. A full page ad stating facts in the local newspaper is a good way to tell your story plus delivering an appropriate health care message. Don't rely on slick printed reports like the Fortune 500 - these should be used for potential donors and to massage your ego.

Employees - don't forget them. Tell them how their hospital is doing and where it is going. Make believe they are your stockholders and give them a written report, a verbal report, and a few refreshments. Allow time for questions - be prepared for some really tough ones. And don't forget the evening, night and weekend shifts.

AUDITORS HAVE A TERRIBLE JOB

I'm not writing about the government auditors (I'll get to them shortly). I'm writing about "The Big Eight" folk. Or should I say "The Big Six" - those firms keep merging and I can't keep track of them.

Anyway, auditors have a terrible job. They perform a vital service, but I don't envy them. Their main responsibility is to the public-at-large. When the public reads a financial statement that is signed by "Ernst, Lybrand & Ross," the public is supposed to have some confidence in the credibility of the financial information.

Who pays the auditors? - the firm that is being evaluated by the auditor. How does the auditor, when faced with a financial mess, fulfill the responsibility to the public *and* maintain a workable relationship with the client who pays for the audit results? It's a dilemma that must bother many people who enter this career field.

One of the ways auditors cope with this problem is to use "wimp language." They try to inform the public, stockholders, trustees, etc. without unduly offending the management of the bad situation. For example, an observation in the auditors' management letter may say, "There should be continued monitoring of the supervisory process in the billing department." Translated, this means the billing supervisor is a jerk and should be fired. But auditors are lovely people and are in the habit of using polite language. When you hire an auditor, I hope you get one that at least verbally can use four-letter words.

During an investigation of the recent S&L debacle, an auditing firm reported "an egregious example of the misapplication of generally accepted accounting principles." "Egregious" - that will send most people scurrying for their dictionary. What the auditors probably wanted to say was, "This is a $165,000,000 ripoff of the public." I'm pleased to note that one of our congressmen described this situation as a "cesspool." CESSPOOL - I understand what that means.

Now for the government auditors. They also have a terrible job. They are supposed to go around to find all the cheaters or potential cheaters of government standards. They are experts at finding doom and gloom, and if necessary, a creative application of government regulations will certainly turn up some bad news.

Imagine spending your career spreading doom and gloom - what an awful way to spend most of your working hours. Why can't they hand out a few compliments of what is going right? Why can't they help shape regulations to assist getting the job done better? They would get much more accomplished with a more constructive (versus destructive) approach.

BE ON TIME

If you are always on time at meetings, please read no further.

Those people who are late to meetings and appointments waste everybody's time - the most precious commodity of any business. Besides, it is *damn rude*. I make a habit out of being on time, and to sit around making small talk while the rest of the group assembles is maddening. When the meeting starts late, the members who have been prompt are seething, and that is hardly the mood for a constructive meeting. If it is the chairperson of the meeting who is late, so much the worse. If you are the chairperson, begin the meeting on time even if only one other person is present.

And *end* your meeting on time. If you don't end on time, you will lose physicians, trustees and other members who count on getting back to their normal job at a certain time.

BEING FIRED

If you are a hospital Chief Executive Officer, you'll find you have an excellent chance of being fired. Of course, if you're not a CEO, you can also be fired.

It's a DREADFUL experience.

Your confidence takes a terrible beating, your ego is shattered, and what will your friends and relatives think? You want revenge. How will you pay your rent? I mean *the sky has fallen.*

Take heart. You're lucky to be out of a bad situation. Go find a new position and avoid the mistakes you made on your previous job.

It will take one to five years to get over the humiliation of being fired, but in a few years you'll be much happier in your new position.

BETES NOIRES

Betes noires are things or people we dislike, but can't do much about. My betes noires used to really bother me, but I've learned to live with them, and at times I kinda like them, because they are my very own. Here are some examples.

1. *Yankees.* When I was a boy my father promised to take me to the World Series if the Boston Red Sox won. I was a loyal Red Sox fan, and each year guess who won the American League - the damn Yankees. I became a rabid Yankee hater, and now that I am older and wiser I still take secret glee when the Yankees are in the cellar.

2. *People who cut in line.* Now this really bugs me, particularly on highways under construction where there are signs to merge into a single lane. Most people merge at the sign, but a few go barreling along the shoulder, and squeeze their car in at the very last minute. I'm always amazed to drive in Canada, because the Canadians all seem to merge at the sign. They certainly have better manners when it comes to queuing up on the highway.

When I get mad at these people, I reflect on a story that occurred during a gasoline shortage when there were long lines at every gas pump. One wise guy passed up most of the line, and got his car wedged in line just before the pump. The lady behind him got out of her car and waved to the other drivers for attention. Then she shouted, "Hey everybody - did you see what a neat job this guy did of jumping in line. Nice going fella! Let's give this guy a great big hand for being so skillful." Then she started to clap, and everyone standing around the pumps and the other drivers, who got out of their cars, began to applaud. They kept this up while he was pumping his gas and glaring at the lady who was leading the cheering section. Someday I'd like to meet that lady.

3. *Coffee cup handles.* Why doesn't someone design a decent coffee cup handle? It takes three fingers to use a coffee cup - the thumb, the pointer and the middle finger. The typical handle works for the thumb and pointer, but the middle finger lacks proper leverage or it gets burned when placed against the hot cup.

4. *Not saying "hello."* When I walk through the corridors of the hospital I usually say "hello" or "hi" to most of the people who pass me. Employees, patients, physicians, salespersons or visitors may not know me from Adam, but most of them smile or nod or return some salutation. However, some people stare at the floor and turn their head away from anybody who passes them and never say hello. These shy or reclusive people are my betes noires.

When I was a shy graduate student at the University of Pittsburgh, I was standing by the entrance to the School of Public Health. A beat up old car drove up, and a scruffy man got out and shuffled into the building. He surprised me with a cheery "Good morning." I quickly mumbled some response. I turned to one of the other students and asked, "Who was that guy?" He replied, "Jonas Salk." Thanks to Jonas, I'm going to continue to say hello, and live with my betes noires.

You'll have plenty of betes noires in your career, and I hope you have as much fun with them as I do with mine.

BIDDING

Bidding is one of the unappreciated art forms of management. It is very complex and takes real talent. Some people are good at it - I'm not one of them.

However, I do know that there are three basic reasons for vendors to submit low bids:

1. A better or equal product produced at a lower cost.
2. A loss leader - the vendor will reduce the profit margin to get your business.
3. Lousy product (lower quality with cheap price).

Avoid number 3 by establishing good specifications and getting good references on the potential bidders.

Number 1 and number 2 are swell, but sometimes you suspect you are getting a number 3.

Our engineer was installing a giant generator in an excavated area. He sent out bids to four companies who did this sort of work. We figured it would require a huge crane and cost about $3500. Sure enough the bids came in at $3600, $3400, $3350, and $1500. Our engineer was suspicious of the low bid and asked the low bidder if he understood the requirements of the job. He said, "Yes" so he was awarded the contract. The following day two truck-loads of block ice were delivered and placed in the excavation. A truck pushed the generator on top of the ice, the ice melted, and the generator was neatly installed. The contractor was smiling as he left the job with a tidy profit. That was a true number 1.

We also had a practice of bidding out the infant formula contract every year. It was a very competitive business, and each year the bids would come in lower. One year a company said they would provide their product at no charge. I was even more amazed the following year when the company *gave us* credit for every case of infant formula delivered. Our hospital had a huge obstetrical service, and we surmised that the mothers who used the formula in the hospital would continue to buy that product once they got home. The formula company would take a loss on the hospital business, but would make ample profits on the volume of sales in the local drug stores and grocery stores - clever.

One other aspect about bidding is the question, "To haggle or not to haggle?" The hagglers like to get in the bids and then go haggle with the vendors to get better terms. The hagglers really enjoy this sport and can point to their successes. I'm a non-haggler. I realize initially I may get stuck with a high price from the vendors. But once you get a reputation of no haggling, the vendors come in with their best offer the first time without a haggle factor added. It may not be as much fun, but in a long run, I believe it results in a better and cleaner transaction.

BILLING

This can be a "job loser" so pay attention.

Most hospitals can perform miracles at saving lives, but they can't send out timely or understandable bills. Millions of dollars are lost by sloppy billing, to say nothing of the reputation of the hospital. Many of our patients are relieved and grateful after their encounter with the hospital - then the billing starts.

The rules of billing are simple:
1. Send them promptly.
2. Be accurate.

During my career I have never seen a hospital bill that I could understand. It is little wonder that our customers get frustrated over the bills. I know we have a complex product, and insurance coverages are complicated, and Medicare, Medicaid and Workers Comp are just as bad; so the inevitable result is a list of procedures and codes that are mystifying plus the computation of the deductibles and co-insurance would challenge the best mathematician. I believe the American public will demand we have national health insurance, not because of all the good reasons the politicians talk about, but just so they won't get any more hospital bills.

At least we can send out bills promptly - or we should. Don't tell me your doctors don't sign the necessary records on time - we are talking about real money and real reputation. If you can't get your bills out on time, either you need a new computer program, a new billing department, or your hospital needs a new CEO.

Here is a true and wonderful story about billing.
When I arrived at a hospital as CEO, I discovered
unbilled accounts up to 5 years old. My new finance
officer and I agreed to write off all individual
accounts that were 3 years and older. Then we sent
out hundreds of bills that were 6, 12, 18 and 24
months old, and then we braced ourselves for the
angry response. Soon I received a phone call from a
gentleman who introduced himself by saying he was
a retired partner from one of the "Big Eight" accounting firms. He noted that he had received a bill
for a surgical procedure done about two years ago,
and he was having a difficult time determining
whether his insurance would cover the expense,
because it happened so long ago. He then asked me
if I knew that my billing department had a problem.
I decided I had better level with this guy, so I gave
him a ten minute dissertation on how we had found
a mess, how much money we'd written off and
acknowledged the risk of sending out bills
that were so ancient.

His response was remarkable. He said, "Oh good!
You know about the problem, and are taking
corrective action. That's how I want my hospital to
be run. Is there anything I can do to help?"

I told him that I anticipated some angry letters-to-
the-editor to be published about our billing procedures, and if they appeared it would be nice if he
could write a response supporting the hospital in its
attempt to correct a bad situation.

He said he would be glad to write such a letter, and
wished me well in my new position.

If he had been in my office, I think I would have
hugged him.

BREVITY

Today we are up to our eyeballs in useless data and wordy communications - a gross waste of human talent.

Practice and preach brevity.

BUDGET CONTROL

"Budget control" is an oxymoron - like "legal brief" and "political integrity."

Most managers believe that budgets control behavior, and most managers are wrong.

Let's take the head nurse on Center A. Does she control the linen consumption, use of the phone, lab tests, meals, drugs, wages, thermometers, electricity, pension plan? NO! She controls her staff, their schedule, their training, their overtime, their assignments, their morale and their vacations.

Don't tell her the pharmacy costs on Center A are too high, because that is a function of physician orders and pharmacy pricing.

Don't tell her the linen consumption is too high on Center A, because that is a function of the illnesses of the patients.

Do tell her to do a good job of supervising her staff, which is the best way to have an effective nursing unit.

Let all your supervisors supervise people, and stop bugging them about the phone costs, equipment repair costs, wages, food costs, and all those other budget items that are out of their control.

CAREER LADDER

We all know career ladders go upward and onward to glory. According to the American business ethic, it is believed that every true blooded American wants to climb up that ladder.

Unfortunately, too damned little attention is paid to those individuals who don't want to climb up anymore, and some of them want to climb DOWN (with dignity).

Not every nurse wants to be the director of nursing or even the head nurse of the unit - Thank God!

Not every accountant wants to be the chief financial officer, but the reverse may be true for some of the older CFOs.

What happens to Dr. Johnson when her term as Chief of Staff is completed?

The message here is: devote enough time to people as they seek to find the next rung of the career ladder, remembering that they may be looking for the next rung DOWN.

CFO

The acronym for chief financial officer is CFO.

Behind every successful Chief Executive Officer (CEO) is a good CFO.

CEOs, and all those aspiring to be CEOs, think they have to master the field of finance in order to be successful. Some worry because they don't know whether the U.S. trade deficit is good or bad. Some worry because they don't understand how Moody's or Standard & Poor's arrive at their ratings for various bond issues. Some lie awake nights worrying about all the idiosyncrasies and machinations of the world of finance.

The smart CEOs have given up worrying about all this stuff, and have gone out and hired a superb CFO - one who can speak in simple English so the CEO can comprehend. So don't fret over your ignorance of the debt/equity ratio. Get a good CFO to explain it to you.

CLEAN

I don't care if you run a post office, a hardware
store, an automobile maintenance garage, or a
library - *Keep it clean.*

It is imperative in the hospital business to keep the
place clean. An easy way to check this out is to
inspect the bathrooms. If they look like a third rate
gas station, you're in trouble.

Speaking of bathrooms, I've often wondered why
there is always a long line of women waiting to get
in the bathroom whenever I go to a concert, fair,
sports event or play. Either there are more women
in attendance or women take longer in the john or
both.

In hospitals a vast majority of the staff are women.
Usually a majority of the patients are women. And
women outnumber men in visiting their friends and
relatives in the hospital. So when you and your
architect design that new hospital, make sure there
are adequate women's restrooms - and keep them
clean.

COMMUNICATION

We communicate in different ways with different degrees of effectiveness. Here are the ratings with 10 the most effective.

RATING	METHOD
8 - 10	Eyeball to eyeball dialogue
6 - 8	Monologue or video presentation
4 - 7	Phone or radio
2 - 4	Memo or newspaper
0 - 1	Not returning phone calls

The best way to communicate is by verbal exchange with accompanying hand motions and body language. If you really want to get your point across, try whispering.

Admittedly you have to document much of your communication in order to reach a broad audience or to make a permanent record. Just don't be surprised if the reader doesn't get the message.

COMMUNITY INVOLVEMENT

Promote community involvement by anyone and everyone associated with your hospital. Your organization should be an integral part of the community, and a fine way to practice this is to participate in its activities. You should set the example by joining Rotary or the scouting program or the Chamber or ..... Encourage the physicians to get involved with providing medical services to the local high school football team or Little League teams, have them join the League of Women Voters, support the symphony orchestra, attend the medical society meetings. Encourage the entire hospital staff to be involved in politics and political issues - no matter what the party or issue. If an employee needs extra time off to run for the school board, provide the necessary flexible schedule and ask her/his colleagues to cover. Have your weekly newsletter praise the community services of the staff.

I once had a cashier in the cafeteria who collected books for the local prison library. She did a great job of getting many of the staff involved in this effort, and made everyone feel good about donating a used book to her program.

Your hospital is a community service - your staff can make it a community citizen.

COMPETITION IS GREAT BUT...

When you shop, when you engage in sports, when you vote, when you watch television, you are enjoying the fruits of competition. The competition may have been for quality, trophies, money, status, beauty, performance, honor, praise or whatever.

The Democrats and Republicans spend most of their energies competing with one another for power, votes, approval, social improvement, national glory, and they do this at the local, state and national levels. BUT if there is a major earthquake, the Democrats and Republicans work together to bring food, shelter, financial support, personnel, etc. to the damaged area.

Shipping companies engage in vigorous competition on the basis of price, volume, delivery capability, speed, etc. BUT if a ship is sinking, all the ships in the area go to help - regardless of competitor status.

Catholics and Protestants have had centuries of competition and regretfully at times have resorted to wars to prove their point. BUT when innocent people were being killed in Ireland in the 1970s, Mairead Corrigan, a Catholic, and Betty Williams, a Protestant, got together to stop this madness. They were awarded the 1976 Nobel Peace Prize for their efforts.

Hospitals compete for patients, personnel, equipment, money, status, etc. BUT when the AIDs epidemic occurred in the 1980s the health leaders had to sit down together to figure out the best way to care for the AIDs patients and stop the spread of the virus.

When times get really tough, collaboration (NOT competition) is required to get the job done.

For the next decade the hospital field is facing some really tough times. We need more collaboration.

COMPUTERS

I only know one thing about computers, and that is:
SOMETIMES THEY DON'T WORK.

So you must plan what to do when that happens.
Decide what information you must have to operate.
If your report on the daily census is four days late -
who cares? The same is true of the budget report.

But let's say your computer is used to cross-match
blood. Now what happens when the computer is out
for four days? You can't say to the patient, "I'm
sorry - you need a couple of pints of blood, but our
computer is temporarily out of action." This is just
one example of many functions that depend on an
immediate response from a computer.

You hold disaster drills on a periodic basis, so don't
forget to run computer disaster drills as well.

CONSENT FORMS

Never read a consent form - just sign it.

When you last took your car in for maintenance or repair, Mr. or Ms. Goodwrench wrote up the problem, gave you an estimate and told you where to sign. I hope you didn't read what you signed. It said that the garage can lose your car, damage your car, not fix your car and it's your fault - or words to that effect. If you don't sign the form, they won't fix your car.

Hospitals are the worst. They have "consent form mania." You have to sign a form that says you will pay for all the costs of your hospital stay promptly without a whimper. You sign a form that says you understand all the risks of hemorrhoid surgery and all the risks of anesthesia and you won't get sore at your doctor if you die. (It took your doctors about 8 years of intensive training to learn their profession and you are supposed to comprehend all of the risks of their work with a five minute explanation.) If you don't sign the forms they won't fix your hemorrhoids.

Not to worry - sign those forms. Get that car fixed or get your hemorrhoids fixed. If they don't fix the problem, and show you your signature on the consent form to "prove" they aren't at fault - that's ridiculous. Any lawyer you hire who is half competent, can show that the consent form is totally irrelevant, because you didn't understand what you were signing.

CONSULTANTS

I hate to hire consultants.

I think it's a problem with my ego, because it means that consultants:

- Know something I don't know (and should).
- Can do a job at less cost than I or my staff.
- Can say things I haven't got the guts to say.

I know the old joke about, "Consultants borrow your watch to tell you what time it is." There may be some truth to that, but nevertheless consultants can be very helpful.

My brother was a consultant on city management. He was engaged years ago by a small Connecticut town to advise them on how to improve the downtown area. His main recommendation was to eliminate all the buildings between Main Street and the small river that flowed through the town. Many of the buildings were partially built over the river and they were unsightly, and they were dumping raw sewerage into the river. When he submitted his report, the City Fathers were appalled at his suggestion, because some of them owned buildings or businesses that were targeted for demolition. My brother was fired. A couple of years later, a major hurricane hit New England, and that little river became a raging torrent and wiped out all of the buildings between Main Street and the river. I always suspected that Mother Nature had read my brother's report.

CONTRACTS

Most contracts are drawn up by lawyers and are incomprehensible. The most important clause of any contract is the escape clause (termination clause or revocation clause). If you don't understand it or agree with it - don't sign the contract.

I've seen contracts with NO termination clause. I've seen a contract where the salary of a physician would continue to be paid to his spouse - even if he was fired or died. I've seen a contract where property would revert to the original owner (a corporation) on the death of the last surviving grandchild of the existing Board of Directors - try keeping track of that mob.

So when reviewing contracts, try to appear intelligent, *but concentrate on that escape clause.*

CONTROL THE PAPER— CONTROL THE MEETING

It's so simple, it's frightening.

The person who controls the paper, controls the meeting.

What are the basic ingredients of a meeting?
- Agenda
- Reports
- Proposals
- Recommendations
- Minutes

They are all on paper.

If you want to control a staff meeting, a stockholders meeting, Congress, a board of directors meeting, a faculty council, a commission - get control of the paper preparation.

Occasionally there is some heated debate at meetings, but it is usually about tinkering with some small portion of a written proposal. There may be some quibbling over minutes. Someone may amend a recommended vote. At worst, an issue gets tabled or rejected for another proposal (the next round of paper).

If you really want wide open committee participation, skip the paper.

If you want total control of the meeting, just prepare reams of documents that no one can possibly digest before or during the meeting.

Some reader is going to observe that I have a low regard for communicating by paper which is inconsistent with this cynical view of controlling meetings (see chapter on Communication).

I'm just telling you how to control meetings - I didn't say I liked it.

CONVENTIONS

Some people think conventions are a waste of money or are boring or both. I like 'em.

The most important reason to go to conventions is to see old friends and maybe meet some new ones. These friends are the people who may help you find a new job ten years from now. They give you tips on where to find a pathologist or a director of nursing or a good resident. They can help get you important committee assignments. They may even help get your kids into college. I hope you reciprocate.

I've heard too many lecturers, because most of what they say, I have heard on previous occasions. Consequently, I am very fussy about what lectures I attend. Usually I select a topic that sounds interesting and I pick up a gem or two, but mostly I learn about what other people are doing about a particular matter that I want to implement back in my own shop. This gives me plenty of information for those nay-sayers back home who are blocking my proposal. Of course I'll neglect to tell them all the reasons that it could be a lousy idea.

The exhibitors at conventions intimidate me. I've always been gun-shy of sales people, because I hate to spoil their enthusiasm with a "no." Some of them invite me to their cocktail parties, which really embarrasses me. The idea that I will buy a product because I've been given free booze has always been an anathema to me. But I am compulsive about wandering through all the exhibits, and am always amazed at the variety of vendors, services and products that are integral to running a hospital.

Lobbying is another adjunct activity of some conventions. Lobbying is part of the "rain dance" of democracy. You should try it. Just to see those mammoth white marble and granite buildings with beautifully furnished wood panel offices is worth the trip up to "the hill." But as you walk through the halls you keep bumping into the Steelworkers Union, the Hog Farmers of America and the Taxidermist Association, and you begin to wonder what is going on. Those poor congressmen have got to listen to the hog farmers and every other private interest group whine about how they need more money, lower taxes, and a national holiday. And to think they run for election to listen to this stuff. I admit I was impressed with the aides of the congressmen who seemed to know what they were talking about. The representatives and senators were polite and attentive, but I thought they probably acted the same way when they met the hog farmers.

Last, but not least, I always take time out to visit the Chicago Art Museum or the Smithsonian or come cultural exhibit in whatever town is holding the convention. It is like playing hookey, which makes it twice as enjoyable. Looking back on these experiences I can remember the museums, but precious little about what went on at the convention.

DISASTERS - BIG ONES

I hope you don't have any big disasters, but you should be prepared. You have drills, and they are helpful; but they don't begin to inform you about the real thing.

So whether it is a fire, a hurricane, an airplane crash, an earthquake or whatever, here are a few tips.

- You will have plenty (too many) doctors and nurses. The word on the disaster will go out rapidly and everyone will want to help. You will even have doctors and nurses from neighboring hospitals volunteering. So don't worry about a lack of professional help.
- Your switchboard will be flooded and frequently useless.
- You will have to rely on pay phones or a few private lines that you should have already installed.
- The media will arrive like a swarm of locusts. Try to keep them out of the patient areas. Set up regular information conferences and give them facts. Hold down on the theatrical presentation - the media folk are able to generate plenty of their own.
- Watch out for burnout. Your staff will work like never before for 24 or 48 hours, and then you can't find people for your normal staffing.
- Make sure your chaplains, psychiatrists and social workers pay attention to the patients and relatives and staff who will probably need plenty of support after the crisis is over.

DOCTOR - SIGN YOUR MEDICAL RECORD!

Getting some doctors to dictate and sign their medical records is a major challenge. You will plead, cajole, threaten, beg, bribe, rant and rave, but some physicians just won't cooperate. It is one of the most childish exercises conducted in the hospital.

The only executive I know who solved the problem was Dick Mastronardi. Dick ran the Social Services Department for the city, and the city hospital was his responsibility. One day the CEO quit, so Dick had to move over and manage the hospital until he could find a replacement. Dick was not familiar with all the peculiarities of the hospital culture. On arrival at his new job, his secretary informed him that he had to sign a bunch of letters to be sent registered mail to the physicians whose failure to sign their medical records threatened their admitting privileges. Dick was aghast. He threw the letters in the wastebasket and told his secretary to call the physicians' offices and tell them they were off the staff if all records weren't signed in five days.

The docs were furious. They were all volunteering their services at this hospital to care for the indigent people of the city at little or no charge. Two of the physicians quit they were so enraged, but the rest came in and signed their records. Dick never had another problem on this issue, and he gained the respect of the remaining members of the Medical Staff for his action.

Too bad Dick didn't stay on as an administrator - he went back to his regular city job and then became a professor at the state university teaching students to care for people (by avoiding the nonsense and bureaucracy of our social institutions).

I don't recommend Dick's approach to the eternal records problem, but I thought you would take some comfort in knowing that one person had solved the problem.

Dogs

DOGS

I'm not talking about people - I'm talking about real dogs. We all know that seeing-eye dogs are essential caregivers to their owners and are allowed in hospitals. Some mental health experts insist that a friendly dog on certain psychiatric units is very therapeutic. Convalescent homes are finding that friendly dogs are very popular with the residents. Indeed, dogs can play a very special role in the health fields.

Some people are worried about dogs carrying nasty germs. Nonsense - they carry dog germs. People carry people germs. If you are worried about nasty germs, worry about the staff, visitors, patients, volunteers, etc.

My favorite dog was HoJo. One evening the hospital received a bomb threat; so I rushed to the hospital to find HoJo and a bunch of cops snooping around the bushes looking for a bomb. I asked why they were looking outside, and one of the officers said, "We can't take a dog in the hospital." I quickly disabused them of this myth, and they took HoJo up to the patient units to do her bomb sniffing. In about thirty minutes HoJo reported no bombs in the area, so we went back to normal operations. I wrote HoJo a personal thank you note in care of the local police department.

I like dogs.

DON'T SWING AT EVERY PITCH

Each day you will be faced with a myriad of problems, opportunities, options, challenges, - whatever. I've seen managers become paralyzed and useless, because they were trying to address all the issues simultaneously, and consequently did a lousy job on all of them.

Learn to be selective, and learn to postpone some matters. I know this will be difficult, because it means that you will have to tolerate a situation that should be corrected. It means drifting (sometimes for years) with a less than ideal operation.

You must develop what has been called "comfort with ambiguity". It may be that three of your most distinguished trustees are all getting senile, or your Emergency Room needs a larger waiting area. It may take months or a year or two to fix these matters; so exercise your comfort with ambiguity.

Learn to swing at those pitches or problems where you have some chance of accomplishing something constructive, and learn to restrain yourself from the temptation of trying to hit a home run at every opportunity.

DRAGONS

Everybody needs a dragon.

Democrats have Republicans (and vice versa).
Women have rights.
Catholics have poverty.
Farmers have drought.
Unions have job security.
Researchers have cancer and AIDs.
The "Big Three" have Japanese manufacturers.
Hospitals have a nursing shortage.
Airlines have lost luggage.
Gardeners have bugs.
The highway department has potholes.

Big dragons and little dragons make life interesting.
Make sure your organization has a few dragons and
each member of your staff has a dragon or two.
Without them you are doomed to a life of ennui and
boredom.

EATING CROW

We all make plenty of mistakes. Most of us hate to admit to them - to ourselves, to others and especially in public.

However there are times when you should acknowledge that you really blew it. This exercise in humility, confession, mea culpa, eating crow (call it what you want) will not only help clear up the mess you've made, but more importantly, the people who hear you own up to the error will respect you for being honest and open.

So don't be afraid to eat crow from time to time. In a short run it may be a difficult experience, but in a long run you'll be glad you did.

Incidentally, when you are eating crow you may want to tell your audience the origin of the phrase "eating crow". Thanks to "Brewer's Dictionary of Phrase and Fable" (Harper & Row, Publishers, New York 1981) we learn the following:

"To eat crow. To be forced to do something extremely distasteful. The expression derives from an incident during an armistice of the Anglo-American War of 1812-1814. A New Englander unwittingly crossed the British lines while hunting and brought down a crow. An unarmed British officer heard the shot and determined to punish the offender. He gained hold of the American's gun by praising his marksmanship and asking to see his weapon. The Britisher then told the American he was guilty of trespass and forced him at the point of the gun to take a bite out of the crow. When the

officer returned the gun, the American in his turn
covered the soldier and compelled him to eat the
remainder of the crow."

EMERGENCY ROOM — the E.R.

If your hospital doesn't have an E.R. it's not a hospital. If you close your E.R.; you just closed your hospital.

I know the E.R. is a financial drain.
I know the Medical Staff shuns responsibility for the E.R.
I know the knife-and-gun club business on Saturday night is grizzly.
I know many patients "abuse" the E.R. with trivial ailments.
I know the homeless use the E.R. when they can't find a shelter or a decent jail.

The public expects (as it should) a hospital to have an E.R.; so make sure you never close it.

One night I got a call at home from the Director of our E.R. saying he was going to close it. I said, "No way!" Then he told me that we had three prison convicts with drawn handguns and three cops with drawn handguns standing in our E.R. I told him, "I'll be right there." I hadn't the vaguest idea of how I could help, but I rushed off to the hospital. By the time I arrived the fracas was resolved - much to my relief. It turned out that a hostage taken during a prison riot was having chest pains. Both the convicts and the cops respected this hostage, so they agreed to a mini-truce to get him to our E.R. The truce included that no weapons would be surrendered. Happy ending - the hostage was admitted to our coronary unit with a minor heart problem. The convicts and the cops went back to the prison and resolved the issues of the riot. And we never closed our E.R.

EMPLOYEE SMARTS

This is going to be tough on your ego - the staff is smarter than you. The sooner you realize this, the more effective you will be as a manager.

When I completed my formal education, I had all the answers. Thanks to a great bunch of people who tolerated me and taught me during my residency program, I found out how little I knew.

Now that I am older and wiser I'm searching for the right questions - I think I'll ask the staff.

EPISODIC CARE

Episodic care occurs when people are hurting and seek help. They react by taking aspirin, alcohol (internal or external), praying, living with pain, crying or all of the above. Most everyone avoids going to the doctor or hospital.

Now we in the health professions are wise and knowledgeable about good health practices, and know that episodic care is foolish. We seek appropriate professional help before or at the first sign of a problem. NUTS - most health professionals avoid doctors and hospitals just like the rest of the public.

The universities teach us that episodic care is bad, and everybody should adopt preventive measures and comprehensive care. This is good in theory, but remember that a vast majority of folk have and will continue to practice episodic care - me too.

Exercise

EXERCISE

You can't manage a hospital or anything else if your body is falling apart. So keep yourself in shape by some sort of exercise.

I'm reluctant to even bring up such an obvious matter, but I learned the hard way, and I hope to save you some grief.

When I started my professional career, I was in great shape having recently been discharged as a pilot from the Air Force. One day, a couple of years later, my boss suggested that I sub for him at his weekly exercise class, which I did. The instructor had a select clientele (mostly company executives and the Governor of the state). The instructor was about 75 years old. We went through some simple floor exercises all in the prone position and after 30 minutes I got a rubdown, a shower and a heat lamp. I drove back to the hospital and could barely get out of the car. I was sore all over. For two days I shuffled around the hospital like some of our sickest patients with everybody snickering at me. It was obvious my boss had set me up to teach me one very painful but effective lesson. Since that experience I have exercised regularly.

I don't care what you do (jog, row, calisthenics, golf, tennis or jai alai) please exercise for the rest of your career, and after if you want to enjoy retirement.

EXPENSE ACCOUNTS

If you work in a government hospital you must play by the government rules on expense accounts. They are awful. You must get a receipt for a taxi ride, a toll, parking, a cup of coffee. No entertaining allowed - like buying a friend lunch so you can talk business. You will have limits on the cost of breakfast, lunch and dinner plus a maximum per diem expense. It is typical dehumanizing ineffective bureaucracy.

If you work in a non-government organization trust your people to use their judgement on travel expenses. The benefits you gain from your employees not worrying about having to play "cheapo" while traveling, and the professional relationships developed on the road will far outweigh the few extra bucks you spend versus the government bureaucratic method.

You may even save some money by not hiring people to process and watchdog all those dinky travel accounts.

FILING

Hospital people love to file things - forever.

- Pathologists keep every glass slide they've ever seen.
- Lawyers tell us to document everything and save it.
- Radiologists like to keep all their old films.
- Medical record librarians keep everything.
- Finance people keep all sorts of outdated data.
- Administrative people each file minutes of all the meetings they attend.

There is just too much being filed away and it costs too much to store. Get everyone to clean out their files. Their motto should be:

WHEN IN DOUBT, THROW IT OUT.

FIRING

One of the really rotten responsibilities you will have is firing people. The reason for firing may be incompetence, cheating, personality conflicts, chemical dependency, senility - no matter what the reason, it's a terrible experience for everybody.

Look at the bright side, most of the time the discharged individual will end up in a much more compatible situation. I know an embezzler whom we fired who got a national award a few years later for his work running a small hospital, and a former CEO who is happy as can be as director of nursing in another hospital. So most of the time you are doing the individual a favor by forcing that person to take on a new role.

You should, whenever possible, help the person locate a new position - in your hospital, in another hospital or in another career. This doesn't mean you should write letters of reference that are untruthful.

FLYING

Some people are scared of flying - me too. I did plenty of flying as a pilot for 4 years in the Air Force, and my business career required plenty more. Maybe I shouldn't say "scared," let's just say I have "profound respect" for a big hunk of metal defying the rules of gravity. Every pilot I know has that same "profound respect," so don't think your pilot is a hot dog or devil-may-care individual.

Here are some tips on how to fly (as a passenger).

1. *Eat regularly.* A few people who are afraid they will throw up on a flight decide not to eat before flying. This is dumb, because an empty stomach may cause you to heave.
2. *Avoid drinking during turbulence.* If you have a cup of coffee or a soda or a martini, and the captain announces, "Please fasten your seat belts, because we may have a little turbulence." - DRINK UP. It is much better to gulp down your drink then to wear it all over your clothes.
3. *Enjoy the view.* It is the greatest benefit of flying, so look out the window. There's a traffic jam on the Los Angeles freeway, ...still some snow on the mountains around Tuscon, the Empire State building is tiny, the farmlands of Ireland are so green, what's that big needle sticking up out of Toronto?...... go ahead and enjoy the scenery and reflect on this little planet of ours.
4. *Go to the bathroom* - before each flight. Hopefully this will avoid that long walk down the aisle with all the other passengers eyeing you with the I-know-where-you're-going look. And you can avoid using those little bitty johns that require the skills of a gymnast to get the job done.

5. *Join the airline club.* If you are a regular flyer,
join one or two of those airline clubs. They
provide comfortable seating, courteous and
quick check-in, free snacks and drinks, tele-
phones and small conference rooms - it's a
bargain. They also help you avoid the waiting
area at the gate where crowds of people are
herded around like cattle.

My favorite airline is Drummond Island Air. John
Danielson and I were flying up to Mackinac Island
in northern Michigan for a hospital convention. We
flew into Pellston and looked around for Drummond
Island Air. There was a sign saying:

WELCOME

Mr. Danielson

Mr. Spaulding

We walked up to the counter, and the receptionist
greeted us and asked for our luggage stubs and
then gave us complimentary beverage tickets at the
restaurant. So we went in for a cup of coffee, and
soon our pilot joined us. He was also the owner of
the airline and a former Air Force colonel. We had
a delightful chat about running a small airline, and
we swapped a few Air Force stories. He asked if we
had been to the island before and we said, "No." So
he extended our 28 mile flight by giving us a tour
pointing out the historic Fort Mackinac, the
governor's mansion, the bike trails and the Grand
Hotel. Then he radioed for landing instructions
and asked them to order a taxi for us.

I was nervous about landing, because I could see he
was going to miss the runway (I was sitting in the
co-pilot's seat). Sure enough, he landed on the
grass next to the runway, and he turned to me and
smiled and said, "I've got to keep up my proficiency
on grass landings, and as a former pilot I knew you

wouldn't mind." He delivered our luggage to the terminal (a little wooden cabin about as big as my family room). Our pilot then confirmed when we wanted to return and wished us a pleasant stay on Mackinac. We then climbed aboard our "taxi," which was a horse drawn carriage (there are no cars or trucks on Mackinac - plenty of horses and bikes).

Who says airlines don't give good service?

GET READY FOR CHAINS

My Webster's says "chains" are:
1. A series of things linked, connected, or associated together.
2. Something that confines, restrains, or secures.

Take your pick.

The chains are coming in banks, bookstores, department stores, drug stores, grocery stores, hardware stores and even hospitals. So long to the independent "Mom and Pop" enterprise. This trend has been going on for years, and there is no sign that it will change. The sooner you recognize that the chains are here to stay, the sooner you will be able to cope with the situation.

To run a business in the 1990's you need:
- Massive purchasing power
- A bevy of lawyers
- A very sophisticated finance department
- Political clout
- Mass marketing
- Modern computer technology
- Access to capital
- International ties

The chains have these things. The independents don't.

The challenge to you is to pick a chain that builds on the attributes of the independent operators, namely good customer relations, quick response to local environment, good employee relations, community involvement, etc.

I hope your chain doesn't "confine and restrain".

GET RID OF THE AX

If you owned a lumbering operation would you use an ax or a chain saw? That's a simple question with an easy answer. The chainsaw gives you more lumber, a fantastic increase in productivity, and happy lumberjacks.

So why do hospitals still use "ax" equipment?

Your staff want to perform well; they want, need and deserve the best equipment.
- Get that new floor polishing machine.
- Install bar coding.
- Buy a new tractor with the gadgets for proper outdoor maintenance.
- Look into the best communication system to the physicians' offices.
- Get modern food carts.
- Provide new and better lab equipment which is being developed every day.
- Keep that software up to date for clerical and financial operations.

Proper equipment means high quality, low cost, and satisfied staff - so get rid of the ax.

GO TO BOTSWANA

If you are an accountant, engineer, nurse, physician or teacher your skills are needed in Botswana. Someday, someone is going to ask you to go to Burma or Peru or Palau to share your skills with the local citizens - *grab the opportunity*.

The local residents may learn something useful from you, they may learn about American culture, and they will probably be most grateful for your help. But the main beneficiary from such an experience is YOU.

Talk to a few people who have had some experience in foreign countries, and you will get an earful about the unusual customs, weird food, climate, ignorance, primitive roads, and the beautiful people they met.

I've been to London, Paris and Vienna and they were interesting and fun, but they were dull compared to the few weeks I spent consulting at the Mercy Hospital in Guyana. I returned from that experience with a new appreciation for:

- Soap ($8.00 per bar)
- The courage of the Catholic Church
- Minority status (3% white population)
- Bread (flour was banned at that time)
- The joy of flying a kite (everyone makes and flies a kite to celebrate the Easter holiday)
- Freedom of the press
- Good health care that can be delivered by dedicated people without fancy technology
- Cricket (the national sport)

I hope you will get the chance to meet and work
with the people of Belize or Nepal or Tunisia. It
will be an enriching (not in money) experience you
will never forget.

GOOD LETTER FILE

In the course of your career you will receive letters telling you what a great organization you have. They are a real pleasure to receive, and of course you should share them with those responsible. Then put them in the "Good Letter File".

You will also receive verbal and written comments on what a rotten job you are doing. At times, this can get very depressing. When some of these negative remarks start to get you down, just reach in the good letter file and read a few of those letters. It will help to restore your perspective and confidence, so you can get on with your job.

HUMOR

A sense of humor is the most under-rated asset of most people - especially leaders.

Just take a minute or two and think about the people you really admire and respect. Winston Churchill is one of my favorites. I can remember some teachers, ministers, physicians, CEOs, assistants, competitors, politicians, editors, and all the good ones had a sense of humor. Not that they were comedians or giggled all the time, but they had a wonderful sense of reality and could deal with adversity thanks to their sense of humor.

I wish the schools could teach how to develop a sense of humor - Humor 101. But it probably comes from your grandparents' genes plus some shaping by your family and elementary school environment.

So when you are recruiting residents, administrative personnel or trustees; look for a good sense of humor. Hopefully you'll find those who can laugh at their own foibles. If they haven't got a sense of humor - too bad. Find someone who does.

IF YOU LOSE A DEBATE—JUST WAIT

I've lost many debates - or thought I did. At the end of a discussion my adversary hadn't moved an inch towards my position. I had obviously failed to get my point across.

If this happens to you - just wait. Maybe two days later or two weeks later your adversary is moving towards your position. Given a little time, she/he is willing to reexamine the issues and rethink the matter. You didn't fail after all. So don't get discouraged if you lose a debate - maybe you didn't.

Of course, this also means that when you think you've won a debate, you may have second thoughts and want to change your position in a day or two.

We lost our chief pharmacist to a very prestigious hospital in the next state. I just couldn't find a qualified replacement, so I called our former pharmacist to ask for help. He said that he had a young man who showed a lot of promise; so we invited him down for an interview with our staff. *The kid was only 28 years old,* and there was no way that I would hire a juvenile to take on the responsibility for a major department. The Chief of Anesthesia told me I was crazy not to hire him. NO SIR - NOT ME! A week later I changed my mind and we hired the kid. He was sensational and soon moved up the ranks of the administrative team. I've always been indebted to that anesthesiologist who planted the seed in my thought process which let me change my mind.

INCENTIVE PAY versus
ANNUAL WAGE

The old American ethic of free enterprise, capital-
ism, greed, or whatever you want to call it, has
spawned an incentive pay system to motivate people
to work harder, smarter, faster, etc. Many hospitals
are adopting this method of paying people based on
certain criteria such as bottom line performance,
quantity of procedures performed, meeting budget
projections, etc.

Most people are still paid an annual wage where
they are told what they will be paid next year based
on longevity, performance, market and cost of living
index. I like this old fashioned method, because I
understand it - I only have to worry about my wage
once each year.

I've watched the incentive pay system work and
seen many flaws. It is usually set up ("gamed") by
management so they make a bonus over the tradi-
tional annual wage. Meeting incentive standards
frequently perverts the real mission of the organization. Statistics are modified, falsified, or arranged
to meet incentive criteria and thus become useless
for management purposes.

I recall a librarian who was in danger of losing her
bonus, because her cost of running her copying
equipment was exceeding the budget. To solve the
problem she put a sign on the copying machine
which said, "Out of Order - Use the Machine in
Administration." The physicians (mostly house
staff) obliged and went to the administrative offices.
When the supervisor found out what the librarian
had done he was enraged, but the librarian said to

him that he set the criteria for the copying equipment and he didn't say how she was to meet his standards.

This is a funny but tragic example of the perversion of the real mission of the organization due to a sloppy incentive pay policy.

I'm not saying that incentive pay is no good, but I am saying it is not effective for many people (like me), and if you do implement an incentive pay program make sure you establish the right incentives and be damned careful to administer it properly.

Internal Warfare

INTERNAL WARFARE

I regret having to tell you this, but most organizations spend too much energy on internal warfare and not enough on getting the job done.

You're going to hear:
- Our President is an airhead.
- If only Mary would fire Jones.
- I think this "new" equipment is government surplus.
- Why can't Finance do anything right?
- Can you believe that Harry got promoted?
- Marketing gets all the money.

It goes on and on, and is very debilitating.

But there is hope, because I have worked in organizations where this internal self-flagellation was almost nonexistent, teamwork was excellent, and we took great pride in our performance. It was fun.

I wish I knew the remedy for internal warfare. If I did I'd tell you.

If you know, please tell me.

IT'S THE LITTLE DOGS THAT BITE

The hospital occupancy is fair, the last inspection
was barely passing, the finances are in rocky shape,
the new physician group is not bringing in patients,
the employees just got a small raise, but no one is
commenting on these matters.

HOWEVER one of your trustees is mad as a hornet
because his wife was not invited to the Auxiliary
picnic. A neighbor wrote a nasty letter-to-the-editor
bitching about the smoke pollution from your
smokestack. The relatives of the patients in the
intensive care unit are sore because there
is no place to put all the flowers which have been
sent to their loved ones. The chief of staff tells you
the carpeting in the lobby is a disgrace.

Just remember, "It's the little dogs that bite".

JEWS ARE SMARTER
THAN CHRISTIANS

At Christmas, the Christians celebrate by exchanging many, many gifts. The kids have opened their 25 presents and really like two of them. The parents are pleased and exhausted. It's over for another year.

The Jews are smarter. They celebrate Hanukkah at the same time, but it takes eight days. A few gifts are given on each of the eight days. Joy for eight days versus one for the Christians.

The lesson here is:
Spread out the good news.

The corollary is:
Bunch the bad news.

Example of bad news:
Let's say you project a major deficit so you are going to lay off 300 employees, hold the line on wages, reduce employee health benefits, and increase rates. You have to get the trustees' support, inform the docs and employees, and tell the public.

Do it all in 48 hours. Don't do it piecemeal!

Example of good news:

Let's say you project a major surplus so you are going to increase pension benefits, start a new cancer screening clinic, raise wages, and hold the line on rates. You have to get the trustees' support, inform the docs and employees, and tell the public.

Stretch out the good news piece by piece. It may take three months before you have released all this good news.

This is nothing very new. In 1513 Machiavelli wrote in "The Prince":
"For injuries should be done all together, so that being less tasted, they will give less offense. Benefits should be granted little by little, so that they may be better enjoyed."

Just like I said:
Spread out the good news.
Bunch the bad news.

JOB DESCRIPTIONS

Job descriptions are another form of bureaucracy that has gotten out of control - way out of control. There is a small group of bureaucrats who worship job descriptions, and every organization has a few of these folk. They think all employees should be hammered into a neat mold (the job description) and held accountable to toe the line on all the descriptive jargon. It is stifling - not only to the employee but to the supervisor.

Fortunately most job descriptions end with the phrase, "......and other duties as may be assigned." That is the most important phrase in the whole job description.

Employees are people, not robots. So don't crush them with the rigid terminology of job descriptions. Let them demonstrate their own initiative, loyalty, hard work, teamwork, and productivity.

Good managers rarely pay any attention to job descriptions - their own or anyone else's.

JOIN

"Americans of all ages, all conditions, and all dispositions constantly form associations." Alexis De Tocqueville, a Frenchman, made this observation in his treatise *Democracy on America* which was published in 1835. I wonder what Alexis would think about the proliferation of today's associations, clubs, commissions and societies.

You're going to have to decide whether, when and which of these associations to join. It is important that you not only join, but also participate in the ceremonies and functions of the organizations. Hopefully your employer will pay for the dues and the conferences, and allow you time off to participate in all the activities.

By joining you are going to meet a group of people with the same problems, frustrations and triumphs that you experience. Sometimes, when you begin to feel overwhelmed by your job, you will discover others in the same line of work have it worse, and then you will feel better about what you are doing. It's the "misery-loves-company" syndrome.

Those associations are also important lines on your curriculum vitae. The people who may want to hire you have some sort of expectation about what associations you should belong to (Chamber, state trade association or national professional society). It gives them some comfort (not necessarily valid) to see a correct profile of associations.

LEAN

The adjective "lean" means: containing little or no fat. It should be the adjective that describes your staff.

A lean staff is hard working - they have to.
They tackle the major issues - no time for trivia.
They work as a team - internal bickering is not allowed.
They are effective - bureaucratic nonsense is scorned.

If you inherit a staff that is fat, trim it down as soon as possible. It won't be easy, but you will find the best performers will shine as the gripers, bureaucrats, and goofoffs are weeded out.

Oh! - one other characteristic of a lean staff. They not only work hard, but they play hard. They really enjoy life, and it's a pleasure to belong to such a group.

"LET'S KILL ALL THE LAWYERS"

I was walking down Connecticut Avenue in Washington D.C., and spotted a coffee mug in a gift shop which said, "Let's kill all the lawyers." What a delicious thought! That would wipe out half the population of our nation's capital and ninety percent of all the politicians. Our troubles would be over - or would they?

I told my lawyer friend about the coffee mug, and he smiled and said that it was a quote from Shakespeare, and I should look it up. So I went to the library and read King Henry VI - Part II. Sure enough - there was the quote. Jack Cade, a common bullying laborer, is thinking of fomenting a rebellion to overthrow Henry and become king. One of his henchmen is Dick, the butcher, who when he hears Jack is going to be king says, "The first thing we do, let's kill all the lawyers."

If Shakespeare were alive today, I wonder what he would write about the legal profession. It seems to me that there are just too many laws and too many lawyers, and every year the numbers increase. But I'll avoid the temptation to get into a diatribe on lawyers.

In the coming years you will be dealing with:
- Contracts
- Liability issues
- Insurance
- Regulation
- Lobbying
- Mergers/Anti-trust
- Bankruptcy
- Collections

- Taxes
- Bylaws
- Personnel policies

to name just a few areas where a good lawyer (law firm) will save you plenty of grief. By "good" I mean a lawyer who knows her/his limitations and has access to other attorneys with the appropriate legal skills.

One last word of caution:
    Good legal advice is expensive.
    Poor legal advice is exorbitant.

Since you can't "kill all the lawyers", at least make sure you hire a good one.

LISTENING

How do you spend most of your waking hours? - Listening.
What did your parents never teach you? - Listening.
What human skill is rarely (if ever) taught in school? - Listening.
What skill is vital to you in your work tomorrow? - Listening.
By listening, I mean the process of receiving sights and sounds and reflecting on them. (Note that listening is much more than "hearing," which is merely the process of receiving sound.) I've read some books on listening, and they don't agree with my definition, so I am baffled by the subject. But I have learned a few things.

1. *On-Off Switch.* We all have an incredible on-off switch. I can turn off traffic noises, snoring, crickets and the whine of jet planes. My wife can hear her kids (or grandchildren) cry, because her switch is perpetually in the "on" position - she accuses me of turning mine "off." At work I am supposed to listen to the same presentation over and over again, so I just flip to "off" and concentrate on something more interesting.

2. *Faking It.* It's so simple. Just look at the person who is talking and nod your head once in awhile. You can be listening to your stomach growl, which means it's time for lunch. My dog is a great faker. He appears to listen to me when I get home from work and tell him what a rotten day I've had. He just sits there and stares up at me with those big brown eyes and gives me an occasional tail thump. I know he's a fake, but I pretend he really is listening.

3. *The Listening Game.* This is a game I play at church, conferences, parties, meetings or whenever a bunch of people get together. I try to figure out who is listening to what and why. It's an interesting way to study human nature, and helps me improve my listening skills. Try it.

4. *Listen to What is NOT Said.* I'm chatting with a friend who just got a divorce. In our conversation there is no mention of the divorce. If my listening is working correctly, I shouldn't bring up the subject. At work I've heard proposals on fantastic business ventures telling me of all the advantages with nary a word on the risks or possible disadvantages. My listening tells me this is a con job.

5. *Listening May Not Involve Talking.* A great example of listening involved one of our vice presidents. Agnes (not her real name) was developing a major bond proposal of several million dollars for a complex capital development program. She was a very bright, tough, dedicated and highly respected executive. Our representatives were at the negotiating table with a bevy of lawyers, accountants, consultants, bankers and of course the officers of the state finance authority. The table was surrounded by three rows of chairs where interested parties could watch the proceedings. Agnes was sitting in the third row. The negotiations went on and on, and things kept getting worse and worse for our corporate position. It was apparent to me that the whole deal was going to fail. At one particular tense moment, there was a lull in the debate, and Agnes got up from her chair and slowly walked up to the first row and sat down. Silence! Then the debate

started again, but now everything was going our way, and the meeting quickly came to an amicable conclusion - to everyone's relief. Agnes never said a word, but those guys were listening.

In Shakespeare's Henry IV, Falstaff admits he has "the disease of not listening." I hope you never catch it.

MBO

Management by objectives, or MBO, is an accepted management technique. You should try to understand it - I have tried and have failed.

The theory seems to be that a supervisor and supervisee(s) sit down and figure out their objectives for the coming year, and twelve months later they will evaluate how they did on those objectives and then develop a new bunch. Balderdash!

The truth is that objectives are developed daily and change frequently. Such as:

Dietician: "I've got to find a way to jazz up the low fat diet menu."

Engineer: "I'm going to see the contractor to see if we can accelerate the renovation project."

Physician: "I should tell the nurses on 3B not to be upset with Bobby Jones' mother. She is a demanding lady, but her demands are understandable given her home situation."

Evaluations should be done daily and as soon as possible. Such as:

Dietician to Chef: "That new low fat diet menu is really well received by the patients."

Engineer to Contractor: "Thanks to you we have moved up the opening ceremonies of the renovation project."

Nurse to Physician: "Thanks for the tip on Mrs. Jones. Now we understand."

The MBO process is much too formalized, and is usually set in an unrealistic time frame. If MBO is such a good idea we should use it to bring up our kids. Just imagine the reaction to:

"Johnny, your room has been a mess for the last twelve months."

or

"Mary, your report card from last June was terrific - nice going."

In dealing with people, we need a little more common sense and fewer stuffy objectives.

MOW YOUR LAWN

If your lawn looks nice (your business lawn - not your home lawn) read no further.

The person who runs a business in a building littered with trash and the lawn and bushes are untrimmed, is *going out of business.*

Imagine a patient going to a hospital to have her/his gall bladder cut out, and seeing that the hospital can't even cut the lawn.

At one state university hospital which I ran, the grounds maintenance was the responsibility of the university maintenance department. Their standard of excellence was to clean the parking lots before and after football games and mow the grass before graduation and the alumni reunion. The hospital lawn was horrible. It looked like the School of Agriculture was using it as a test weed patch. I finally prevailed upon the superintendent of maintenance to mow our grass weekly. He grumbled about his budget, until I told him I would get the chancellor to give responsibility for the hospital grounds to the hospital, and get his budget reduced. I admit his staff did an excellent job once they understood the hospital's needs.

NAME TAGS

There's a world of difference between name tags and
security badges. Security badges are used by the
armed forces to prevent espionage. They have little
photographs of the bearer sealed in plastic so the
military police can tell if you are a spy.

NAME tags are designed so other people can read
your name. Patients need to see names, not dinky
photographs. Patients are exposed to many, many
technicians, housekeepers, aides, dieticians, docs,
nurses, receptionists, cashiers, etc., and they want
to identify you by name.

Here are some examples of patients' reaction to
illustrate why name tags are important:
1. Security badge: "The cute nurse told me that
   I could have pain pills
   anytime I wanted."
   Name tag: "Doctor Maple said I could get up
   and use the john today."
2. Security badge: "The black maintenance man
   was very courteous and
   thoughtful."
   Name tag: "Brenda somebody-or-other was
   very rude to me in the admitting
   office.
3. Security badge: "It was a middle aged woman
   with a funny hairdo who took
   my rings away for
   safekeeping."
   Name tag: "Ms. Jones from administration
   stopped by to ask if everything was
   satisfactory. Wasn't that nice."

Patients and relatives want and need to communicate. Help them by having readable name tags and
get rid of those silly security badges.

NEWSPAPERS

There are two cardinal rules about newspapers:
1. Never debate with a newspaper.
2. Never lie to a newspaper.

During your career, newspapers will make erroneous statements about your institution, quote you out of context, and even impugn your character. Your first temptation will be to enter into a debate to correct the errors or insults. Restrain yourself. Newspapers thrive on controversy, and if you keep the debate going, you'll be sorry. Newspapers always have the last word, so chances are you will lose any and all debates. The vulgar rendition of this rule is:
"Never get in a pissing contest with a newspaper."

Don't lie. There will be times when you are tempted to give out a little misinformation - nothing malicious, but you have stretched the truth a tad. When newspapers find out about this (and they will) you are in for plenty of grief. A friend of mine released some information to a major national newspaper which promptly gave it glorious coverage plus a fantastic editorial. Within a few days the editors discovered the information was flawed so they looked very foolish, and the editors were very angry. They didn't print a retraction. Instead they assigned their best reporters to dig up anything controversial about the hospital. A few months later the newspaper had a front page series for five consecutive days (plus editorials) on all the scandalous issues of the hospital.

It just doesn't seem fair that newspapers can dump on your operation, but you can't dump on their operation. Who said newspapers were "fair"?

"NO"—USE IT

"No" is a perfectly good word. It was probably the first word you ever learned. So why can't more managers use it more often? Many managers know when to use the word, but only the good managers use it.

Don't shilly-shally with, "Let me think about that." Don't say, "That's interesting - let's do a study." Don't weasel out by saying, "I'll check with our attorney."

Just say, "No." The people who made the request will respect your answer and probably expected it.

Here are some practice requests for you to consider.
- The Womens' Auxiliary wants to buy a new rug for your office.
- Won't you give an extra $300 to the PAC?
- Let's purchase a travel agency and set it up as a money making subsidiary.
- Will you head up a committee to study our property taxes?
- Let's have one more drink.

Did you get the correct answers?
No
No
No
No
No

NURSES

If there was a decathlon event in the health field, nurses would win every contest. They act as pharmacists, chaplains, admitting officers, obstetricians (when the real ones are late), anesthetists, social workers, dieticians, plumbers, managers, housekeepers, computer operators, secretaries, and besides this they give the patient most of the care.

They work in the operating room, nursing units, emergency room, hospice program, clinics, telephone answering service, schools, industrial infirmaries, home health agencies, and the Peace Corps.

They are overworked and underpaid with dreadful working hours and high stress jobs.

Their services are so essential that I'm not sure you can do much about their work, their hours, or their stress, but you can damn sure make certain they are properly compensated - with respect and money.

Of course nurses don't have all the answers. One night Sophie, the night nursing supervisor, called me at home and said, "A crate of live turtles was just delivered to the door of the emergency room. What should I do?" I quickly responded, "Check to see if they have Blue Cross." Sophie, who wasn't known for her sense of humor, didn't think this was funny at all. So I told her to get the aides to put the turtles on the receiving platform and give them some water. The next morning the receiving clerk delivered the turtles to the school of nursing for the anatomy class.

O CANADA!

There are many similarities between the Canadian and U.S. health systems. Both have the same profile of diseases, the hospitals are organized the same way, the professional associations are identical, and the universities teach the same material.

The major difference is that the Canadian system is BETTER!

* The Canadians spend about 30% less for their health care versus the U.S. citizens.
* The Canadian federal government, the provinces, and the health professions all work together to make the system better, versus the adversarial relations in the U.S. between the professions, states, and the Feds.
* Everybody in Canada has health coverage versus about 45 million U.S. residents who have nothing.
* Canadians can go into nursing homes at no fee versus the U.S. where many citizens have to go into bankruptcy to qualify for long term care.
* The Canadian problem with medical liability is minuscule compared to the U.S.
* The Canadian health indicators (death rate, morbidity, etc.) are superior to the U.S.

I think the U.S. should join Canada. It would solve two of the greatest problems of the U.S.
1. It would give the people in the U.S. a superior health system overnight.
2. It would give the U.S. a glorious and inspiring national anthem they could be proud of - O CANADA! and replace the current star spangled anthem to which no one can remember the words or carry the tune.

1/3 1/3 1/3 RULE

This rule applies in all organizations.
ON ANY GIVEN ISSUE:
   1/3 are performing superbly
   1/3 are adequate but can do better
   1/3 are poor performers and won't or can't do
   much about it.

As an example, let's look at the XYZ Hospital
system made up of six hospitals - A, B, C, D, E and
F.

On the issue of financial performance they rank as
follows:
   A+B have strong bottom lines
   C+D are struggling but showing a small profit
   E+F are losing their shirts

On the issue of community relations they rank as
follows:
   E+D are doing great
   A+F are doing O.K. and are trying hard
   B+C don't understand the issue

On the issue of quality emergency services they
rank:
   A+F are terrific
   B+E have a satisfactory E.R.
   C+D are doing a lousy job

Note that there is a different ranking depending on
the issue; so the "flagship" on one issue may be the
"Titanic" on the next issue.

Now the question is where does the XYZ Hospital
System spend its energy to address these issues?

The recommended approach is:

Top 1/3 - Don't mess with them except to hand out kudos and maybe get them to help the middle third.

Middle 1/3 - Chances are that these folk can improve with some assistance, so give them a helping hand.

Bottom 1/3 - If you can tolerate the situation leave them alone - it takes too much energy to make a little progress. But sometimes you have to make a gargantuan investment of resources to fix an unbearable mess.

OUR KIDS ARE TALLER—SO WHAT?

The kids of my generation are over one inch taller than their parents - and my generation is taller than our parents. It doesn't take a genius to figure out that people are getting taller.

This has major consequences for hospitals. It means that beds are going to get longer. This means that rooms must be bigger so the guerney and all the other medical equipment can maneuver in the patient's room.

If you visit an older hospital most of the rooms are dinky. That's because the person who designed the room ignored the fact that we're growing taller.

When you design your hospital, don't saddle the future staff with dinky rooms.

PAC

This chapter is going to tick off plenty of people - at least I hope it does.

A PAC (political action committee) is a bunch of people who collect money to give away to politicians so they will vote for legislation that supports the interests of the donors such as labor laws, farm subsidies, sale of weapons, and environmental issues. In the health field this has been going on for almost twenty years.

Over that period of time I have noticed that the greater the PAC handout - the greater the chance of rotten legislation.

Every year I would dutifully make my donation to my friends who were "putting the arm" on me for the PAC, and every year I would see the hostility of our elected officials increase.

Recently I called the office of a state senator from my district to see if he wanted to attend a dinner honoring some health workers in the community. I thought this might be a nice gesture. His aide said he might consider the invitation if a $3000 contribution would be forthcoming. WHOA! What's going on here?

I keep reading in the media how PACs are corrupting our democratic process. I hear politicians saying their judgement is not influenced by PAC contributions. And each year the AMA and the NRA and the rest of us make record contributions - at the federal and state levels.

This is madness.

I think the AHA (American Hospital Association) should lead a reform movement, and do away with PACs at all levels of politics. Maybe we could go back to debating how best to distribute health resources instead of debating how to distribute PAC funds.

PARKING

Lotsa luck!

Remember that:

- Most doctors want to park in the lobby.
- Clergy love to have special parking.
- Important people (like you) like to have some special area - it helps their ego.

Whatever you do is usually wrong, so don't lose any sleep over the eternal parking dilemma.

PARTIES

There are times for celebration:
- The Christmas/Hanukkah party
- Annual meeting(s)
- Anniversary or birthday of the organization
- Picnic for families
- etc.

Some people would prefer to see the dollars spent on celebrations moved instead to their paycheck, but celebrations and traditions are important.

Just make sure that the committee to organize the affair is made up of the troops. You can stay out of the planning, and just do what you're told to do.

PHYSICIANS

Physicians are troublesome, weird, independent, childish, aggravating - I like 'em.

It took me fifteen years to figure out that fighting the docs was really dumb and working with them can be really fun. I'm a slow learner.

So here are some pearls of wisdom I've picked up about the medical professions.

1. All doctors are *very* smart. They had to be in order to get into medical school. Given the facts about a problem, they can usually come up with a pretty good solution. The trick is to give them the facts. However, they are so darned busy that they haven't got time to listen.

2. All doctors eat. When eating, they like to discuss things not related to their practice like Wimbledon, the real estate market, or the latest scandal in Congress. They will listen at mealtime. So hold your meetings with the docs over breakfast, lunch, coffee breaks, cocktails and hors d'oeuvres, or dinner.

3. Physicians have different personalities. Certain types seem to gravitate to a particular specialty. Different specialists relate differently to administrative matters. Here are some generalizations about some of the specialties from an administrator's viewpoint.

Surgeons: If you need bold decisive leadership get a surgeon. They tend to see all options as "good or bad" - "right or wrong." They will get the job done and aren't bothered about "stepping on a few toes."

Internists: If you need a thinker, a statesman, a facilitator - get an internist. They have excellent understanding of all the issues and all the options. Sometimes they are perceived as pedantic by their colleagues.

Family Practitioners: They are tough to find because they are too busy scratching out a living. If you can get them to devote some time, they usually have a superb understanding of the issues and have a good perspective on the medical staff and how it works - or doesn't work.

Pathologists and Radiologists: They have enough administrative headaches of their own and would just as soon not take on any more.

Anesthesiologists: They get excellent training by refereeing between the surgeons and the O.R. nurses. They are good at solving administrative matters if you can pry them out of the O.R.

Pediatricians: They not only treat patients, but they spend most of their energies relating to very troubled parents. Thus they have a good perspective on management problems.

Obstetricians: I never could figure out this bunch.

Psychiatrists: They think about patients, drugs, families, sex, cultures, legal matters, history, relationships, etc. They are very sympatico with management matters. Sometimes they are perceived as being a little crazy by their colleagues.

House Staff: Their youth, naivete, enthusiasm are refreshing. Involve them in administrative affairs if possible. They will learn to appreciate some of the complexities of organizational life, which will benefit their future careers - and yours.

4. Never generalize about physicians.

PLANNING AND PLANNERS

Planning is important, and planners are important; but the REAL plan is in the head of the CEO (and a few other leaders) and not in that 200 page document titled "Long Range Plan - St. Mary's Hospital 1992 - 1997." Planners compile these documents to show population projections, market share trends, age profile of physicians, and other boring data.

The real plan might be:
- St. Mary's Hospital wants to close the competing hospital, because this community needs only one hospital. Merger is the first option.
- Our anesthesia department is lousy; so we'll force the chief into early retirement and hire that new professor from the University to turn our anesthesia program into a first class operation.
- Two years from now we should run a slight deficit to show the local politicians we need better funding. It should be easy by improving our pension program, which we should have done a couple of years ago, and it should be well received by the employees.
- The President of the new manufacturing company is a real go-getter. Let's put her on the Board of Trustees before the other hospital gets her, and ask old Mahoney to accept emeritus status - his hearing is getting even worse and he rarely attends meetings - nice guy, but he is over the hill.

Now let's face it, these things aren't going to be documented, and will only be discussed within the key leadership group. These are the issues that will really set the strategic direction of the hospital.

PRAISE IN PUBLIC

Praise is a great motivator - it motivates everyone.

Do it as much as possible.

Tell the individual or group directly.

Then tell their friends, co-workers, family, etc.

You can even broadcast good performance in the media.
> We used to take out an ad in the local newspaper picturing the employee of the month, which showed what neat people we had and, consequently, what our value system was all about.

The Corollary: Discipline in private!

PROFESSIONAL ODDS

Different professionals have different mind sets, so it is not surprising that there is sometimes difficulty in communicating. Here are the odds on how four professionals view each opportunity.

PROFESSION	ONE CHANCE IN:
Insurance Agent	1000
Lawyer	100
Finance Officer	10
CEO	2

Example:
The ABC Hospital in Beaufort, South Carolina is considering the construction of a radiation therapy wing. This is how the professionals approach this opportunity.

Insurance Agent: What happens if there is an earthquake and radioactive material contaminates the inter-coastal waterway? We must insure against the enormous cost for environmental cleanup.

Lawyer: Doctor Jones will be in charge of this unit so we have to commit Jones to a five year contract to protect our investment. But Jones may turn into an alcoholic, so we've got to be able to get rid of Jones. This is going to be a tricky contract to prepare.

Finance Officer:	The managed care plans are growing and are cutting out any fiscal surplus. The Congress is nattering about radiologists making too much money; so they probably will reduce our reimbursement in the future. This is a very risky venture.
CEO:	All of the residents of Beaufort now travel to Savannah for their cancer therapy - over a one hour drive. If we can serve them right here in Beaufort, we'll probably increase our other services as well, such as chemotherapy, lab, inpatient census, etc. This proposal has a decent chance of being successful. WE'LL DO IT!

QUALITY

Everybody is talking about "quality."

It's an elusive concept - at least it is to me.

All disciplines have their own criteria for what is "quality," and most of the criteria are incomprehensible. I've given up trying to understand all the complicated definitions of "quality."

The only one that ever made any sense to me was:
DO IT RIGHT THE FIRST TIME.

So if you are
- Making a diagnosis
- Cleaning the floor
- Writing a memo
- Pinning a hip
- Making soup
- Giving an injection
- Fixing a leaky faucet

you get an A+ if you do it right the first time.

QUESTIONNAIRES

First I want you to answer this question.
> The quality of the paper on which this book
> is published is?
> _____ Excellent
> _____ Satisfactory
> _____ Poor

Ha! I'll bet you've never thought about the quality of the paper of anything you've read in the last year.

So why do you ask your patients a bunch of questions they haven't even thought about? Here are some examples:

- Was the admitting process satisfactory?
- Was your room clean?
- Was the food served at the correct temperature?
- Did you receive a prompt response to your call button?
- Was the air conditioning in your room comfortable?

Why not give the patients the opportunity to comment on whatever *they* want to. That way you are going to get some valid responses. Give them a self-addressed envelope (no stamp necessary) form to mail to the hospital with a space to comment on their stay, and a "thank you for your response." Even better, have someone phone the patients at home and ask what they thought about their hospital stay.

You are going to get some real responses like:

- No one told me when to change my bandage.
- My room was filthy.
- Susan Holmes is the best nurse in the world.
- Your bills are totally incomprehensible.
- I nearly froze in your X-ray department.

Now you have something you can work with.
- Tell Holmes how terrific she is.
- Check the temperature in Radiology or remind the staff to put a blanket on all patients going to Radiology.
- Etc., etc.

Throw out all those questionnaires which just give you useless data.

RACIAL PREJUDICE

I've had it all my life. I guess everyone has some bias about different races.

I used to think the French were a scurvy bunch, but one day my mother told me that half my ancestors were French - I've had to rethink my position, and now I believe the French are O.K. people.

I never had any opinion about the Finns - I never met any or learned about their history. Since then I have worked with five Finns, and they were all fantastic. So now I have a strong racial bias *for* the Finns.

My prejudice about Blacks and Hispanics has gone through all sorts of changes - I hope in the right direction. But despite my attitude, I believe hospitals (and most other businesses) have done an awful job of recruiting Blacks and Hispanics into the health careers. Somehow we have to do better, and a good way to start is to ensure they have plenty of educational opportunities.

REGULATORS

Most hospital people think regulators are a pain in the neck. But they have a broad, long range, objective viewpoint, and thus are an essential thread in the health care fabric, and don't you forget it.

Regulators are dedicated, underpaid, and hate to be bulldozed by political pressure - although they have to deal with it on a routine basis. So avoid the temptation of exercising your political muscle to beat the regs.

Regulators have great memories. If you think you've slipped something by the regulators today, brace yourself because the regulators may "throw the book" at you two, five or ten years down the road.

The truth is that regulators have a good track record of being right (versus managers); you may not like dealing with regulators, but you had better learn to listen and respect them.

RELATIVES

Not yours - the patient's.

Many of them are rude, unreasonable, obnoxious, and repugnant. Chances are they are going to wind up in your office telling you what a crummy hospital you run. They have already blasted the nurses and doctors about the food, lack of treatment, tests, personnel, costs, admitting, pain, air-conditioning, - everything is rotten.

This used to bother me.

Then a wise old physician gave me some good advice. He noted that this is common behavior for relatives who are guilty of not having given enough attention or love to their relative (the patient) and want to compensate by criticizing everyone and everything in the hospital.

He said to listen carefully and acknowledge their concern for the patient. They are troubled people and need your support. It works.

Further, it has helped me to be more reasonable when my relatives have been in a hospital.

RETIREMENT—WHO CARES?

The concept is simple - set aside some money during the working years, so you can enjoy the retirement years. However, fulfilling this dream is very complex and centers around the question of "Who cares?"

1. *The Kids.* In most of the world the family is a tightly knit unit, so the working kids care for their parents (and grandparents). But during the 20th century western civilization and in other more affluent countries, the family unit has become dispersed, and the elderly have increasingly become self dependent (not all good, but not all bad). The working kids now keep in touch with their parents, but they have their own financial worries, particularly bringing up their children and saving for their retirement.

2. *Uncle Sam.* The federal government set up a program called Social Security in the 1930s, and Medicare and Medicaid in the 1960s. These programs provide a foundation to support the elderly in their years of retirement. They are important programs, particularly to people with lower incomes. The feds have also set up tax abatement programs and established protection standards for company pension plans. Sam cares.

3. *The Unions.* Defining the needs of retirement for their members has been a major accomplishment of the unions in the 20th century. They have set the pace for many government initiatives and for non-union business as well.

4. *The Employer.* This subject is usually a very tough decision for the employer, namely what kind of pension or saving plans to offer employees. The options are infinite and range from generous to zero. Hopefully your employer will:
   - Engage reputable firms to design and administer the programs.
   - Use a group of the most respected and brightest employees to oversee what's going on.
5. *You.* The most important piece of the retirement equation is you. Only you know if you want to work until you are 75 or quit the rat race at 55. Only you know if you want a castle in Spain (with a yacht for traveling), or a mobile home in Florida close to good surf fishing. Only you know if you are going to inherit a half a million bucks or just the gold watch that Grandpa Ned got when he retired years ago.

I've checked out some books from our local library on this subject. Most of them tell me how I should have invested my money 25 years ago. The inspirational books tell me all about the opportunities I now have to really enjoy life and not to sit there and watch TV. Heck - I enjoyed watching TV.

You (secretary), and you (CEO), and you (electrician) - please remember to care for you.

ROMANCE

There is romance in every kind of business, but hospitals are the champions. By romance I mean where men and women get together.

There is an abundance of literature, movies and TV shows that use the hospital as the setting for some pretty steamy emotional entanglements. It's no wonder with people running around half undressed. The poor patients have to wear those silly pajamas that tie behind the back and do little to maintain a sense of privacy. Many of the employees wear scrub suits and gowns that expose more than they conceal.

Hospitals are indeed in a body contact business. There is physical therapy, needles poked in various parts of the anatomy, back rubs, tubes inserted in various orifices and that cold stethoscope running up and down your back and chest, not to mention all the activity that takes place in the operating room. It is high tech and high touch. Perhaps more importantly hospitals are in an emotional contact business. The drama of the emergency room, the fear of some terminal disease, the mental aberrations of the psych ward and the joy of delivering twins are examples of the high emotional experiences characteristic of hospitals. This involves patients, doctors, families, technicians, clergy and almost every employee in the hospital.

I know there is plenty of hanky-panky that goes on in hospitals, but I also know of many examples of patients, relatives, employees, students and professionals who have developed long and lasting relationships with one another - true romance.

I had a patient complaint about this subject that baffled me. The patient was a young man who had been in an automobile accident and was confined to bed in a body cast with a frame and pulleys to provide some mobility. His complaint was about the nurses who, when they would stretch up to hang his intravenous bottle, would reveal their under-garments. This was in the days of mini-skirts, so I wasn't surprised by his observation. He said I shouldn't allow the nurses to wear mini-skirts. I thought he was kidding, but *he was serious.* The last thing I wanted to do was to get in a debate with the nursing department on the "proper" length of their skirts. The best advice I could give the young man was to look the other way when they hung up his I.V. bottle. I doubt if he took my advice, but I can report he had a full recovery after a couple of weeks in the hospital.

ROOM WITH A VIEW

When patients are convalescing do they want a
room with a lovely view? - NO!

Do most *healthy* people want to relax in a room with
a lovely view? - Yes.

The ideal view for the patient would be overlooking
the entrance to a brothel or the emergency room or
a children's playground or even a parking lot or the
loading platform. They want to see some action. As
soon as patients get out of their room, they want to
be at the core of activity, which is usually the
nurses' station. They can look at a colorful garden
or a beautiful mountain scene for about two minutes
before getting bored.

So save the nice view for the employees' cafeteria,
because these busy people need to know there is a
world of serenity outside the hectic pace of the
hospital.

Beware - most architects don't understand this. If
they refuse to believe it, tell them to sit in a chair
and stare at a beautiful garden for a few hours.

SECRETARIES

Some people say, "Secretaries are unnecessary, and the new personal computers have made secretaries obsolete."

"Some people" are wrong!

A good secretary can do more for the quality of life of her/his boss than anybody else in the organization. So get yourself a good one.

I've had fantastic good fortune during my career of getting great secretaries. Here are some examples of their attributes.

- They have the ability to greet an angry visitor and after a few minutes of conversation have the visitor in a calm, reasonable and sometimes genial frame of mind.
- As historians, they can recall past meetings and incidents that are key to the resolution of a current issue. I have been spared untold grief by my secretaries reminding me of pertinent past events.
- My mail would arrive with suggested response to some of the correspondence. Those responses were accurate, courteous and appropriate, and usually superior to the answer I would have made.
- Thanks to my secretary's role as travel coordinator, I've flown out of cities after a major snowstorm when most people were still in line at the ticket counter or listening to the busy signal of the airline reservation phone number.
- A keen sense of humor has rescued me from my emotional highs and lows with such remarks as, "Who put gravel in your breakfast food this morning?" or "Buck up, worse days are coming."

Any manager who believes a personal computer can replace a secretary is missing one of the greatest joys of her/his career.

SECURITY PEOPLE

When looking for good security people for a hospital, hire retired police personnel. Right? - WRONG!

The correct answer is to hire retired personnel from the fire department. The reason is very simple. Firemen (epicene word) have a career of saving lives and promoting safety - the same value system as most hospitals. In my experience they relate well with people, are in good physical condition and are happy in a hospital environment while supplementing their retirement pay.

Retired cops are O.K., but their career has been spent "getting the bad guys" - hardly the mission of the hospital. Of course if your hospital is in a tough neighborhood and you experience plenty of crime and violence, hire a few retired cops.

SISTERS (NUNS)

I used to be afraid of sisters - still am.

I worked for a group of sisters for over ten years, so
I know what I'm talking about. I'm not Catholic, so
I'm very objective about the whole subject of sisters.
I take that back - I'm subjective.

In the first place, they start off their meetings with
a prayer, usually asking for God's help in their
deliberations. This always struck me as an unfair
advantage for Catholic organizations, because the
other organizations I worked for never lined up God
on their side when they held meetings.

They're sworn to obedience. Some people interpret
this as "submissive" to the rules of the Catholic
Church. Obedient - Yes. Submissive - No. Most of
the sisters I've met love the church. In fact they
love it enough to object to the twaddle and puffery
that emanates from the official ranks of the
Church. This dissent is probably uncomfortable for
the hierarchy, but it is what makes the Church a
dynamic a vibrant force in today's society.

Professors, lawyers, administrators, politicians,
ethicists, doctors - sisters are playing key roles all
over the world. I wonder why they aren't members
of the clergy.

Some swear, cheat at golf, smoke, play poker, tear
up parking tickets and drink too much - like the
rest of us.

I'm still in awe of their dedication, humor, power, mystique, humility, life styles and value systems. The hospitals in Australia, Canada, Guyana, Ireland, U.S. and many other countries are darned lucky to have them. The same goes for their schools and universities and any other mission the sisters choose to perform.

SPORTS

Sports are a key dimension of corporate culture - don't neglect them. If you have five minutes to read the newspaper before going to work, don't read about the stock market - that just goes up and down and nobody knows why. Read the sports section. When you get to work you will be conversant on what most of your colleagues are talking about. If you don't know whether the local team won or lost yesterday, you might as well "call-in-sick," because nobody is going to talk to you.

You don't have to be a sports nut and be a walking encyclopedia of baseball trivia going back to 1876. You don't have to run the Super Bowl pool (but you should buy a $2 chance). You should know that some super athletes make millions, and you can translate that knowledge into the economic theory of "supply and demand." You should know that some college athletes are almost illiterate, and then wonder about the value system of our educational establishment. You should know that an unusually large number of strikes are called to coincide with the deer hunting season.

If you go to foreign countries, do a little research into their sports mania. Learn about soccer if you go to Argentina, bicycling in France, and ping-pong in China. I was fortunate to join a consulting team going to Guyana - a beautiful but very poor country. About one third of the Guyanese play cricket and the rest are cricket fans. Cricket is a form of baseball that takes forever. When we were there we got to play cricket with a bunch of kids, and after that experience, our rapport with the Guyanese improved 100 percent.

So while you are working on economic trends and modern management practices, take time out to enjoy the international pastime - sports.

SUITS

I've got more than 100 suits.

Three of them are cloth, and I own them. The rest are all legal documents at some stage in the lugubrious process of our judicial system.

The first time I was named in a suit against our hospital I was devastated. As time went on, I found out I had plenty of distinguished company in many of the suits - the mayor of our city, the governor of the state, and the Secretary of Health, Education and Welfare (now the Department of Health and Human Services). I suppose I'm awfully cynical about this very complicated legal process, because so much energy is spent by seemingly intelligent people such as judges, investigators, insurance adjusters, recorders and lawyers in this game of suing. Not only do they spend their own time, but they involve nurses, medical record librarians, managers and physicians in countless hours of paperwork, waiting in court, testifying, etc. Sometimes the process takes years - it's disgusting.

We had a secretary named Chris, who went to our emergency room one evening, and a physician put a needle in the back of her hand and hit a nerve by mistake. She lost the use of her right hand, so she couldn't type. If this had happened on the job, Workers' Compensation would have settled the matter in a few days. *We advised Chris to get a lawyer and sue us.* We would have made a quick settlement to help Chris. She wouldn't do it. She said, "You're my friends - I can't sue you."

We argued with her but to no avail. She stayed on the job, and typed with one hand. We got her to physical therapy, and after about nine months she had regained most of the mobility in her right hand.

There are many people like Chris - in fact most people are like Chris. But more and more the great suing game is thriving. In short, we are becoming a litigious society - what a waste.

If we could only adopt a no-fault system like Workers' Compensation for medical liability. It would be an enormous improvement over the present legal morass. Then I suppose we would have to worry about all the unemployed lawyers.

I just hope the next generation figures out a better way to compensate and care for people who are injured by the mishaps of the health system.

SUPPORT YOUR LOCAL SCHOOL SYSTEM

Perhaps no two sectors of social services are as intertwined as education and health. If you get the opportunity, support your local educational system.

WHY? Because:
1. Your employees in the clerical, dietary, house keeping, maintenance, and technicians are likely to be graduates of your community school system. The basic skills you need are founded and found in that system.
2. Professionals (docs, nurses, psychologists, scientists) like to live in a community with an excellent educational opportunity for their kids and themselves.
3. Your patients and public learn their basic health value system in large part in the schools.

One other thought occurs to me about our educational system. If you are looking for trustees, check out the talents of the school administrators. They have a superb grasp of community, media, politics, marginal financing, professional idiosyncrasies, wages - most of the issues inherent to hospitals.

TELEPHONE ANSWERING

Here is a chart to describe the caller's response to the length of time it takes to have their phone call answered:

NUMBER OF RINGS	CALLER RESPONSE
1 or 2	Surprised and pleased
3 to 5	No reaction one way or the other
6 to 10	Frustration and building anger
Over 10	Ready to kill

The message is clear - answer promptly.

No matter what the caller wants to communicate, it will be more effectively accomplished with a prompt answer.

In one hospital I joined, the head surgeon stormed into my office and told me it took 32 rings to get the switchboard to answer his call to schedule a surgical procedure. He was properly enraged. Later in the week I met with the supervisors' committee and confirmed that this was a problem for everyone and had been for years. Was it the equipment or lack of personnel? I asked the supervisors to work on the problem, and the following day the chief telephone operator asked me if all the employees and staff could do their own direct paging instead of always going through the switchboard. I said, "Sure." Evidently my predecessor had a rule that only the trained operators could use the paging system.

One week later the hospital was responding to calls by the second ring. The paging process was quick and effective. Everyone was delighted with the new system - particularly the operators who had been taking abuse for years, and now they were being appropriately praised.

I left that hospital a few years ago, but occasionally have reason to call. I'm happy to report I have yet to wait more than two rings.

TIME CLOCKS

Time clocks are dehumanizing and were inherited from olden days. If you have them in your organization - GET RID OF THEM.

Sure a few people will cheat on filing their work hours, sick time and vacation, but peer pressure and good supervision should control the cheaters.

Occasionally a group of employees will request a time clock, and in this case it is O.K. to have them; but you should test this request every year or two with the troops.

TOP LINE versus BOTTOM LINE

Everyone talks about "the bottom line" as if it were the Holy Grail. Balderdash!

The top line is far more important and don't forget it.

The top line defines your mission:
    Hospital - cares for the sick
    Grocery store - sells food
    Library - lends books, tapes, etc.
    Airline - flies people where they want to go

The bottom line is merely a momentary financial score of how your business is doing.

If you concentrate and work on the top line, chances are you will get a good bottom line.

If you concentrate on the bottom line, chances are you will neglect the top line - and blow it.

TOUR TOUR TOUR

This applies to hospital CEOs, but most managers are responsible for some area of their organization so this applies to your turf as well.

Got 15 minutes? - Tour
Got 40 minutes? - Tour
Got thirty minutes after church on Sunday? - Tour

Where to tour
Mostly patient areas - especially the emergency room. Don't forget the:
> Kitchen
> Stores
> Lab
> Maintenance
> etc., etc.

How to tour
1. Greet patients, staff and visitors with, "How's it going?"
2. Listen
3. Listen
4. Listen

Why tour
1. You'll learn things you would never learn in your office. Like:
   - The walls in the Coronary Care Unit are finally being painted.
   - Ms. Washington, who does the baking, is a Red Sox fan.
   - Most staff and patients think Dr. Martin is GOD.
   - Harry, your best electrician, is quitting in a huff.
   - Margaret, the new O.R. tech, had twin girls.

2. People like to see you. Some want to talk to you. You may find this hard to believe, but they do.

So for the rest of your career - Tour, Tour, Tour.

TRAIN AND PROMOTE

Good managers train people to seek new horizons and help them get there.

Lousy managers try to recruit good people and won't let them go.

New employees want to belong to an organization that will enhance their skills and provide new opportunities. So what if your new talented assistant moves over to a competing hospital - you now have a friend in that hospital. If you have a reputation of "training and promoting" you will always have an abundance of the best and brightest applicants.

When an employee wants to apply for another position in the hospital (or even in another career field outside the hospital) a good manger will help them try something new. The bad manager will look at this as an act of desertion and try to obstruct the transfer. They even get sore at the new supervisor who is accused of "stealing" employees.

Train and promote - you'll never regret it.

TRUST

Trust: assured reliance on the character, ability, strength, or truth of someone.

Here is a vital quiz question:
How many of your employees do you trust?

_____ All
_____ 95%
_____ 75%
_____ 50%
_____ None

If you answered "All" - you're naive. There are a few rascals in every organization.

I hope you answered 95%, because that means you work in a good outfit. Your management style and policies should reflect this trust. If you are directing all your energies to weeding out the cheaters (rigid personnel policies, frequent reports, inspections) you are neglecting the real performers. Let peer pressure take care of the "bad guys," and support the 95%.

If you answered less than 95%, get another job. You're in the wrong organization.

TRUSTEES

Each health organization has its own set of criteria when it comes to selecting trustees, so it is difficult to generalize, but I'll do it anyway.

1. The key characteristics of any trustee should be:
   - Intelligence
   - Decent value system
   - Experience (banker, school board member, politician, editor, etc.)
2. Selection of a trustee primarily because of race, religion, sex, or politics is unfortunately necessary in some cases, but try not to ignore #1 above.
3. Doctors are new on most boards of hospitals. Most of them think they "represent" the interests of the Medical Staff—big mistake. Explain to them that bankers don't represent the interests of the banking industry, but should have some cogent thoughts on finances. Doctors should have some cogent thoughts on where the hospital is going—which at times conflict with physicians' interests.
4. Attendance at meetings is nice but not crucial. I had a trustee who rarely attended meetings, but when times got really tough, this individual could facilitate the solution with a couple of phone calls.
5. Someone noted that it takes a minimum of three years before a person is an effective trustee—I concur.
6. A few trustees will want to meddle in management. It is inevitable, so brace yourself

and try to minimize this problem.
7. Prepare the chairperson of the board prior to each meeting—spell out the controversial issues, the directions which are most desirable, personality conflicts, and try to avoid any surprises.
8. The more social interaction you have with the trustees, the better.
9. Before making any major media announcements, inform your board. They hate to appear uninformed.
10. Participation in deliberation is normal. But I knew one trustee who *never* entered into any debates and would always go along with the recommended votes. One day, on a very sensitive matter, we presented our recommended course of action, and this individual softly asked, "Why?" Everyone present was shocked, and the matter was quickly tabled. On further study, we reversed our recommendation. This was one of the best trustees I have known.
11. Start your board meetings on time, and more importantly end on time.

TYPOS

I used to tolerate typos. It just wasn't worth the
hassle to do the letters and memos all over again.

Then a friend of mine (only really good friends tell
you this kind of thing) said to me that I looked like
an idiot when I sent out correspondence with typos.

Either I was sloppy, illiterate, careless or didn't give
a damn - or all of the above. The same went for my
secretary.

Since that helpful criticism - NO MORE TYPOS.

*   *   *   *   *   *

If you spot any typos in this book - no excuse. I may
be sloppy and careless, but I do give a damn and I'm
sorry.

UNMARKETING

"Unmarketing" is the flip side of marketing. They don't teach this subject in the "B Schools," because it is such a shabby subject.

I travel in Canada and have witnessed interesting examples of marketing and unmarketing. If you buy toothpaste, grass seed or ketchup (catsup) in Canada the labels are printed in both English and French. Obviously the ketchup people want all Canadians to buy their ketchup. That's marketing.

But there are many shops and signs that use ONLY English or French, which is a subtle (or not so subtle) way of saying the proprietor doesn't care about serving the English speaking customer or the French speaking customer. That's unmarketing.

I recognize the language debate in Canada is very complex and at times ugly, but as a visitor from "the States" it seems a shame these two rich cultures can't work together in a little more harmony.

Hospitals are also experts in unmarketing. I know of a hospital (which shall remain nameless) that was having a problem with the increasing number of poor people using their emergency room services. To solve the problem, the administrator *reduced* the size of the already crowded waiting area. The poor people in the neighborhood then had to go to the other hospitals for decent service. That's unmarketing!

Unfortunately unmarketing is a strategy for many of our social services, and I don't want to single out hospitals. I'm sure you can think of several examples of the shabby practice of unmarketing.

VACATIONS

I get very nervous when I hear someone say "I haven't taken a vacation in five years." Translated that says:

- I don't trust my staff.
- I am a martyr.
- I neglect my family.
- I'm afraid my skulduggery will be revealed if I'm gone.

Even the sincere workaholic should take a vacation. It will do her/him good to have a change of pace and get away from the hassle of business. It will preserve their sanity, help their home life, and give them a fresh outlook on their work.

Make sure your people are taking vacations. You too.

One day in October I was sitting in my office, and my boss walked in. He plunked some keys down on my desk and said, "Here is a map on how to get to my cottage, these are the keys, and I don't want to see you for a week." Before I could respond he walked out. When I recovered, I called my wife and told her to pack the car for one week on Cape Cod. It rained most of that week and was terribly cold, but it was probably the best vacation we ever had - walks on the beach, jigsaw puzzles, fire in the fireplace, reading, and the kids loved it. Now THAT was a vacation.

VENDORS

Software, beds, legal services, orange juice - how do you get the best? Each vendor gives you a big sales pitch on the merits of their product. How do you get the real story?

It's simple. Ask two questions.
1. Who are your competitors?
2. Why is your product better?

Now you will get the whole truth and hear such remarks as:
- The XYZ company has lousy service in this area.
- XYZ loads their food with salt.
- Their guarantee is only good for one year.
- Their firm has limited experience with state regulators.
- They have a limited choice of colors.

No product is perfect, so you should find out the limitations - don't ask the vendor to knock their own product, because they won't do it. Ask their competitor.

VOLUNTEERS ARE WONDERFUL— WATCH OUT

Volunteers love to volunteer. They like to work (for no pay) for a cause, an institution, a community service - it makes them feel good about themselves and the mission they are supporting. They get our politicians elected, run the Boy Scouts and Girl Scouts, and are a vital force in most hospitals. They operate the gift shop, help supervise the pediatric nursery, greet patients, and sometimes lobby the state legislature (very effectively I might add). They raise money through various projects (the annual Follies, dinner dance, bake sales, etc.), and they are most supportive during major fund raising campaigns, sending a clear message to their neighbors, friends and relatives to give generously. Furthermore they recruit summer volunteers from students on vacation, who frequently go on to various health careers.

But volunteers aren't perfect, so watch out. Their availability is limited to times convenient to them - not the hospital. They don't have to be team players and frequently don't give a damn about authority. Sometimes their goals vary or are counter to the goals of the hospital. Some employees resent volunteers for taking their jobs away or leaving the employees with the lousy work hours or the dirty details of the job.

Here is a true story with a happy ending. We had a group of volunteers who would buy equipment for the hospital that they, the volunteers, wanted - not what the hospital needed. They enjoyed buying bassinets, heart monitors, and laboratory gadgets - usually some doctor put them up to it. One day a dietary helper was telling a volunteer how she was searching for scholarship support for her daughter to study violin at the local Music College. You guessed it - the volunteers set up a tuition scholarship fund for the hospital employees with the enthusiastic backing of the administration. The awards were based on family income, and the fund was administered by a group of employees and volunteers. From that day on our employees knew those volunteers were wonderful.

You constantly have to remind volunteers that they work for the hospital - not the other way around.

WASTEBASKETS—USE THEM

Wastebaskets are the most neglected, under-rated, and under-used equipment in today's business world.

For just a few bucks you can have a nice one.

Here's a list of things needed to get you started in the proper use of the wastebasket:
- Policy manuals
- Budgets
- Job descriptions
- Long range plan
- Daily reports
- Organization charts
- Minutes of meetings

Once this is accomplished, you have removed the paper straight jacket of your organization, and your staff will be free to move forward.

If I could give an award for the most useful piece of management equipment in the 20th century, it would not be the copy machine, fax, computer, or telephone. The wastebasket would win hands down.

WHAT IS THE ANSWER?

In my career I had several sinking spells because I didn't know the answer to a series of problems. Like:

- Which is the best hospital bed and why?
- How do I get $30 million in capital?
- Where do I find a good bacteriologist?
- Which systems should be operated by the auxiliary generator?
- What should be the food costs per patient day?

The list goes on and on. I still don't know the answers to those questions.

One day I confessed my ignorance to my mentor, and he said, "You don't have to know the answer, but you do have to know *where to find the answer*." And I did know that - purchasing agent, lawyers, bankers, search firms, chief engineer, Joint Commission, dietician, trustees, health department, controller, American Hospital Association, physicians, vendors, etc. - they are the people with the answers.

So don't get depressed when you don't know the answer; instead concentrate on WHERE to get the answer. It's really very simple.

WHEN ANGRY...

There will be times when you want to explode because someone has really screwed up - badly. Your first impulse is to kill or to write a letter blasting the culprit. Go ahead and write that letter - it will make you feel better. *BUT DON'T MAIL IT.*

Go home and "sleep on it" - if you can. Come in to work the next day and read that letter, and I'll bet you throw it in the wastebasket.

Twenty four hours and a good night's sleep will help you to figure out a more reasoned response to the situation. It might even be a good idea to do a little investigation before you respond.

WHERE IS YOUR ICONOCLAST?

Don't run for your dictionary.
ICONOCLAST: one who attacks established
beliefs or institutions.

O.K. - now where and who is your iconoclast?

Everyone needs an iconoclast, and certainly every business needs an iconoclast or two or three or more. Universities, political bodies, the Fortune 500, and most hospitals go through periods of puffery, and they need somebody to point out all the phoney nonsense that is being enshrined by the institution. The modern terminology for these individuals is "skunks." They will probably make your life miserable today, but your business will be the beneficiary in the long run.

Plato in his *Apology* remarks:
"I am that gadfly....and all day long and in all places am always fastening upon you, arousing and persuading and reproaching you."

Gadfly or skunk or iconoclast - cherish them.

WOMEN

Who gives most of the health care in the U.S.?
WOMEN!

Who used to control, direct, govern and manage
health care in the U.S.? Not women.

Who is going to control, direct, govern and manage
health care in the U.S. in the 21st. century?
WOMEN!

In the old days, the old boys club used to dominate
completely all the positions of leadership, money,
and power. Administrators, physicians and trustees
consisted mostly of males - sometimes exclusively.
The same is true of Congress, large corporations,
colleges, etc. But times are changing rapidly in the
health fields, and by the 21st century women will
outnumber men in almost every category. Just look
at the number of women in the graduating classes of
the schools of business, medicine and public health,
and it doesn't require any genius to figure out that
soon women will be running the show.

Although you may call me a "male chauvinist," I do
believe that women have a lower tolerance for the
old boys club traditions and trivia, and therefore we
can look forward to different *and better* leadership
in the next century that will result in better
healthcare.

"YOU DON'T NEED MORE MONEY"

"Work smarter"
"Get the fat out of the system"
"You don't need more money"
"We've got to do more with less"

There is some truth to these statements - but not much. Usually they are uttered by politicians and managers who don't know how to solve a problem, and aren't willing to devote the energies and resources necessary to find the solution.

If we are going to:
- Clean up our environment
- Fly to Mars
- Have decent education for our kids
- Care for the growing elderly population
it will require more money.

So when you are tempted to mouth off one of those above mentioned trite phrases, think again.

YOU HAVE MET KATIE

You may not realize it, but you have already met your "Katie."

One day a hospital CEO asked me if I knew Katie Smith (not her real name). She was one of the best trustees of this neighboring hospital, and I was introduced to Katie. It turned out she was my best girlfriend during my college days until she dumped me for some other guy at another college. It was an amicable breakup, but I was devastated. After our reintroduction, Katie and I worked on a number of joint projects for her hospital. She is now the trustee representative for the state hospital association, and doing a marvelous job.

You have met your "Katies" in high school, scout troop, the armed services, church or somewhere. During your career you will be amazed at how many times former acquaintances will turn up in your professional life, so avoid making enemies in all your social activities.

YOUR TURN

A few people want to communicate with the author of a book about their reactions. You may be one of those people. Here's your chance.

I've made it easy for you.

On the following page is a letter that you can use to put down your reactions.

Whit Spaulding
6397 Sunningdale
Birmingham, Michigan 48010

Dear Whit,

Your chapters on

_____

_____

_____

were fantastic.

However, the ones on

_____

_____

_____

were dreadful.

Why didn't you write about the following subjects?

_____

_____

_____

Your dog, Barn, could have written a better book.
_____ Strongly agree
_____ Probably
_____ Nah

Sincerely,

Name: _____

Address: _____

_____

WRITING IS LIKE PROSTITUTION
FIRST WE DO IT FOR LOVE
THEN WE DO IT FOR FRIENDS
THEN WE DO IT FOR MONEY
            -Moliere

Order Form

Name   _____

Address: _____

              _____

I wish to order:

A Deer In The Lobby
            $9.95 (Paperback)
            $17.95 (Hardcover)

Quantity   Price X Quantity

_____ $ _____

Michigan Residents
add 4% sales tax $ _____

Shipping Cost of $2.00 $ _____2.00_____

Total amount of check is $_____

Mail Check or money order to:

        Whit Spaulding
        6397 Sunningdale
        Birmingham, MI 48010

Signature: _____ Date:_____

Notes

Notes

Notes